Lindy West is a Seattle-based writer, editor and performer whose work focuses on pop culture, feminism, social justice, humour and body image. Her column for the *Guardian* has legions of devoted readers, hungry for her bold and provocative prose. She contributes opinion pieces to the *New York Times*, and was formerly a culture writer for *GQ* magazine and a blogger for feminist site *Jezebel.com*. With followers from all over the world, West's tweets and online articles are a catalyst for global conversation, generating thousands of comments and shares.

@thelindywest
www.lindywest.net

# shrill

**NOTES FROM A LOUD WOMAN**

# LINDY WEST

Quercus

First published in Great Britain in 2016 by
Quercus Editions Ltd

This paperback edition published in 2017 by

Quercus Editions Ltd
Carmelite House
50 Victoria Embankment
London EC4Y 0DZ

An Hachette UK company

A CIP catalogue record for this book is available
from the British Library

PB ISBN 978 1 78429 554 7
Ebook ISBN 978 1 78429 555 4

Every effort has been made to contact copyright holders.
However, the publishers will be glad to rectify in future editions
any inadvertent omissions brought to their attention.

Quercus Editions Ltd hereby exclude all liability to the extent permitted
by law for any errors or omissions in this book and for any loss,
damage or expense (whether direct or indirect) suffered by a third
party relying on any information contained in this book.

Portions of the following chapters were previously published in
different form: The Red Tent in *The Stranger*; The Day I Didn't Fit
in *Jezebel* and the *Guardian*; and The Beginning in the *Guardian*.
Certain names and identifying characteristics have been changed,
whether or not so noted in the text.

10 9 8 7 6 5 4 3 2 1

Text designed and typeset by Jouve (UK) Milton Keynes

Printed and bound in Great Britain by Clays Ltd. St Ives plc

*For Dad*

# Contents

# Contents

# Shrill

# Lady Kluck

Why is, 'What do you want to be when you grow up?' the go-to small talk we make with children? 'Hello, child. As I have run out of compliments to pay you on your doodling, can you tell me what sort of niche you plan to carve out for yourself in the howling existential morass of uncertainty known as the future? Also, has anyone given you a heads-up that everyone you love will die someday?' That's like waking a dog up with an air horn and telling it that it's president now. 'I don't know, Uncle Jeff. I'm still kind of working on figuring out how to handle these weird ice pops with the two sticks.'

There was a time, I am told, when I was very small, that I had a ready response to the question. The answer was ballerina, or, for a minute, veterinarian, as I had been erroneously led to believe that 'veterinarian' was the grown-up term for 'professional animal-petter'. I would later learn, crestfallen and appalled, that it's more a term for 'touching poo all the time featuring intermittent cat murder', so the plan was abandoned. (The fact that ANY kid wants to be a veterinarian is bananas, by the way – whoever does veterinary medicine's PR among preschool-aged children should be working in the fucking White House.)

That period – when I was wholly myself, effortlessly certain, my identity still undistorted by the magnetic fields of culture – was so long ago that it's beyond readily accessible memory. I do not recall being that person. For as long as I can recall, any time I met a new adult – who would inevitably get nervous (because what is a child and how do you talk to it?) and fumble for that same hacky stock question – my imagination would come up empty. Doctor? Too gross. Fireman? Too hard. Princess? Those are fictional, right? Astronaut? LOL.

While we're interrogating childhood clichés, who decided that 'astronaut' would be a great dream job for a kid? It's like 97 per cent maths, 1 per cent breathing some Russian dude's farts, 1 per cent dying, and 1 per cent eating awesome powdered ice cream. If you're the very luckiest kind of astronaut ever, your big payoff is that you get to visit a barren airless wasteland for five minutes, do some more maths, and then go home – ice cream not guaranteed. Anyway, loophole: I can already buy astronaut ice cream at the Science Centre, no maths or dying required. Lindy, 1; astronauts, nada. (Unless you get points for debilitating low bone density, in which case . . . I concede.)

Not that it mattered anyway. Astronaut was never on the table. (Good luck convincing a fat kid that they should pursue a career in floating.) Thanks to a glut of cultural messaging, I knew very clearly what I was not: small, thin, pretty, girlish, normal, weightless, Winona Ryder. But there was precious little media telling me what I *was*, what I *could* be. For me, 'What do you want to be when you grow up?' was subsumed by a far more pressing question: 'What *are* you?'

I'd squint into the future and come up blank.

What do you want to be when you grow up?

I can't tell. Static? A snow field? A bedsheet? Sour cream?...Is sour cream a job?

As a kid, I never saw anyone remotely like myself on TV. Or in the movies, or in video games, or at the children's theatre, or in books, or anywhere at all in my field of vision. There simply were no young, funny, capable, strong, good fat girls. A fat man can be Tony Soprano; he can be Dan from *Roseanne* (still my number one celeb crush); he can be John Candy, funny without being a human sight gag – but fat women were sexless mothers, pathetic punch lines, or gruesome villains. Don't believe me? It's cool – I wrote it down.

Here is a complete list of fat female role models available in my youth.

## Lady Kluck

Lady Kluck was a loud, fat chicken woman who took care of Maid Marian (and, presumably, may have wet-nursed her with chicken milk?!) in Disney's *Robin Hood*. Kluck was so fat, in fact, that she was nearly the size of an adult male bear. Being a four-hundred-pound chicken, she wasn't afraid to throw down in a fight with a lion and a gay snake\* (even though the lion was her boss! #LeanIn), and she had monstro jugs, but in a maternal, sexless way, which is a total rip-off. Like, she doesn't even get to have a plus-sized fuckfest with Baloo!†

---

\* 'Gay snake' felt kind of weird, so I texted my friend Guy Branum.

    **ME:** Is it problematic to refer to Sir Hiss as a gay snake?

    **GUY:** He's super gay. He exists in the tradition of insidious gay dandies.

    **ME:** That's still fucked up, though. Is Prince John gay? Wait, is Jafar gay???

    **GUY:** Jafar is super gay. Prince John is effete and incompetent. Scar is gay.

    **ME:** Those are all the exact same character! They even have the same voice! Disney is the worst.

    **GUY:** Pop culture is the worst. Disney only uses character tropes we've seen before. We gays are unnatural and preoccupied with power. A common theme here is conniving outsiders trying to steal the game – manipulate the system to gain power/protection the non-noble way. Grima Wormtongue, all Jews, gays, women who gossip or do anything but be pretty and passive.

    **ME:** I'm so grossed out by how aggressively Disney trains children to defend traditional straight 'alpha male' authority.

    **GUY:** It's changing.

    **ME:** We are fun at parties.

† I know that this bear's name is technically Little John. But Little John is clearly a character being played by a bear actor named Baloo, who also played himself in *The Jungle Book* and, decades later yet seem-

(It's weird that motherhood is coded as sexless, by the way. I know most of society is clueless about the female reproductive system, but if there's one thing most babies have in common it's that your dad goofed in your mom.)

## Baloo Dressed as a Sexy Fortune-Teller

In order to assist Robin Hood in ripping off Prince John's bejewelled decadence caravan, Baloo adorns himself with scarves and rags and golden bangles and whirls around like an impish sirocco, utterly beguiling PJ's guard rhinos and incapacitating them with boners. Baloo dressed as a sexy fortune-teller luxuriates in every curve of his huge, sensuous bear butt; self-consciousness is not in his vocabulary. He knows he looks good. The most depressing thing I realized while making this list is that Baloo dressed as a sexy fortune-teller is the single-most positive role model of my youth.

## The Queen of Hearts

I do not even know this bitch's deal. In *Alice in Wonderland*, her only personality trait is 'likes the colour red', she doesn't seem to do any governing aside from executing minors for losing at croquet, and she is married to a one-foot-tall

---

ingly un-aged, in *Tale Spin*. (Sub-theory: Baloo is the thirteenth Doctor.) I'm calling the bear Baloo and this conversation is over.

baby with a moustache. She is, now that I think about it, the perfect feminazi caricature: fat, loud, irrational, violent, overbearing, constantly hitting a hedgehog with a flamingo. Oh, shit. She taught me everything I know.

## That Sexual Tree from *The Last Unicorn*

This fine lady was just minding her biz, being a big purple tree, when Schmendrick the garbage sorcerer came along and accidentally witchy-pooed her into a libidinous granny. Then he's all mad when she nearly smothers him twixt her massive oaken cans! Hey, man, if you didn't want to get motorboated to death by a fat tree, you should have picked something thinner and hotter to transform into your girlfriend. Like a spaghetti strand, or a clarinet.

The sex-tree that launched a thousand confusing fetishes taught me that fat women's sexuality isn't just ludicrous, it's also suffocating, disgusting, and squelchy.

## Miss Piggy

I am deeply torn on Piggy. For a lot of fat women, Piggy is it. She is powerful and uncompromising, assertive in her sexuality, and wholly self-possessed, with an ostentatious glamour usually denied anyone over a size 8. Her being a literal pig affords fat fans the opportunity to reclaim that barb with defiant irony – she invented glorifying obesity.

But also, you guys, Miss Piggy is kind of a rapist? Maybe

if you love Kermie so much you should respect his bodily autonomy. The dude is physically running away from you.

## Marla Hooch

*A League of Their Own* is a classic family comedy that mines the age-old question: What if women... could do things? Specifically, the women of *A League of Their Own* are doing baseball, and Marla Hooch is the most baseball-doingest woman of them all! She can hit home runs and run bases and throw the ball far, all while maintaining a positive attitude and dodging jets of Tom Hanks's hot urine! The only problem is that she is not max bangable like the other baseball women – she has a jukebox-like body and makes turtle-face any time she is addressed – which, if you think about it, makes her not that good at baseball after all. Fortunately, at the end, she meets a man who is ALSO a jukebox turtle-face, and they get married in a condescending-ass ceremony that's like 'Awwwww, look, the uglies thinks it's people!' (Presumably they also like each other's personali – What? Doesn't matter? Quarantine the less attractive? 'OK!!!)

The thing about Marla Hooch is that the actress who plays her is just a totally nice-looking regular woman. I always think of this thing Rachel Dratch said in her memoir: 'I am offered solely the parts that I like to refer to as The Unfuckables. In reality, if you saw me walking down the street, you wouldn't point at me and recoil and throw up and hide behind a shrub.' Hollywood's beauty standards are so wacko that they trick you into thinking anyone who isn't Geena Davis is literally a toilet.

## The Neighbour with the Arm Flab from
*The Adventures of Pete & Pete*

Big Pete and Little Pete spent an entire episode fixated on the jiggling of an elderly neighbour's arm fat. Next, I didn't wear a tank top for twenty years.

## Ursula the Sea Witch

The whole thing with Ariel's voice and Prince Ambien Overdose is just an act of civil disobedience. What Ursula really wants is to bring down the regime of King Triton* so she and her eel bros don't have to live in a dank hole

---

* I HAVE SOME QUESTIONS ABOUT KING TRITON. Specifically, King, why are you elderly but with the body of a teenage Beastmaster? How do you maintain those monster pecs? Do they have endocrinologists under the sea? Because I am scheduling you some blood tests. While we're on the subject, a question for the world at large: What is the point of sexualizing a fish-person? It's not like you could really have sex with King Triton, because FISH PENIS. I don't think fish even have penises anyway. Don't they just have, like, floppy anal fins that squirt out ambient sperms in the hope that lady-fishes will swim through their oops-cloud? *Is that really what you want from your lovemaking, ladies?!* To inadvertently swim through a miasma of fin-jizz and then call it a night? A merman is only a hottie with a naughty body *if you are half attracted to fish.* In conclusion, IT'S A FUCKING FISH-MAN TRYING TO DRAG YOU TO THE OCEAN FLOOR,

tending their garden of misery slime for the rest of their lives. It's the same thing with *The Lion King* – why should the hyenas have a shitty life? History is written by the victors, so forgive me if I don't trust some steroidal sea king's smear campaign against the radical fatty in the next grotto.

## Morla the Aged One from *The NeverEnding Story*

A depressed turtle who's so fat and dirty, people literally get her confused with a mountain.

## Auntie Shrew

I guess it's forgivable that one of the secondary antagonists of *The Secret of NIMH* is a shrieking shrew of a woman who is also a literal shrew named Auntie Shrew, because the hero of the movie is also a lady and she is strong and brave. But, like, seriously? Auntie Shrew? Thanks for giving her a pinwheel of snaggle-fangs to go with the cornucopia of misogynist stereotypes she calls a personality.

## Mrs Potts

Question: How come, when the teapot and cup turn back into humans at the end of *Beauty and the Beast*, Chip is a

---

WHERE IT PLANS TO USE YOUR DEAD BODY SEXUALLY. KILL IT. IT HAS A FORK.

four-year-old boy, but his mother, Mrs Potts, is like 107? Perhaps you're thinking, 'Lindy, you are remembering it wrong. That kindly, white-haired, snowman-shaped Mrs Doubtfire situation must be Chip's grandmother.' Not so, champ! She's his mom. Look it up. She gave birth to him four years ago. Also, where the hell is Chip's dad? Could you imagine being a 103-year-old single mom?

As soon as you become a mother, apparently, you are instantly interchangeable with the oldest woman in the world, and/or a pot of boiling brown water with a hat on it. Take a sec and contrast Mrs Potts's literally spherical body with the cut-diamond abs of King Triton, father of seven.

## The Trunchbull from *Matilda*

Sure, the Trunchbull is a bitter, intractable, sadistic she-monster who doesn't even feel a shred of fat solidarity with Bruce Bogtrotter (seriously, Trunch?), but can you imagine being the Trunchbull? And growing up with Miss Effing Honey? The world is not kind to big, ugly women. Sometimes bitterness is the only defence.

That's it.

Taken in aggregate, here is what I learned in my childhood about my personal and professional potential:

I could not claim any sexual agency unless I forced

myself upon a genteel frog; or unless, as part of a jewel caper, I was trying to seduce a base, horny fool such as a working-class rhinoceros; and if I insisted on broadcasting my sexuality anyway, I would be exiled to a sea cave to live eternally in a dank garden of worms, hoping that a gullible hot chick might come along once in a while so I could grift her out of her sexy voice. Even in those rare scenarios, my sexuality would still be a joke, an oddity, or a menace. I could potentially find chaste, comical romance, provided I located a chubby simpleton who looked suspiciously like myself without a hair bow, and the rest of humanity would breathe a secret sigh of relief that the two of us were removing ourselves from the broader gene pool. Or I could succumb to a lifetime of grinding pain and resentment and transform into a hideous beast who makes herself feel better by locking helpless children in the knife closet.

Mother or monster. Okay, little girl – choose.

# Bones

I've always been a great big person. In the months after I was born, the doctor was so alarmed by the circumference of my head that she insisted my parents bring me back, over and over, to be weighed and measured and held up for scrutiny next to the 'normal' babies. My head was 'off the charts', she said. Science literally had not produced a chart expansive enough to account for my monster dome. 'Off the charts' became a West family joke over the years – I always deflected, saying it was because of my giant brain – but I absorbed the message nonetheless. I was too big, from birth. Abnormally big. Medical-anomaly big. Unchartably big.

There were people-sized people, and then there was me.

So, what do you do when you're too big, in a world where bigness is cast not only as aesthetically objectionable, but also as a moral failing? You fold yourself up like origami, you make yourself smaller in other ways, you take up less space with your personality, since you can't with your body. You diet. You starve, you run until you taste blood in your throat, you count out your almonds, you try to buy back your humanity with pounds of flesh.

I got good at being small early on – socially, if not physically. In public, until I was eight, I would speak only to my mother, and even then, only in whispers, pressing my face into her leg. I retreated into fantasy novels, movies, computer games, and, eventually, comedy – places where I could feel safe, assume any personality, fit into any space. I preferred tracing to drawing. Drawing was too bold an act of creation, too presumptuous.

When I was about 8, I was at a birthday party with a bunch of friends, playing in the backyard, and someone suggested we line up in two groups – the girls who were over one hundred pounds and the girls who were still under. There were only two of us in the fat group. We all looked at each other, not sure what to do next. No one was quite sophisticated enough to make a value judgement based on size yet, but we knew it meant something.

My dad was friends with Bob Dorough, an old jazz guy who wrote all the songs for *Multiplication Rock*, an educational kids' show and *Schoolhouse Rock*'s maths-themed sibling. He's that breezy, froggy voice on 'Three Is a Magic Number' – if you grew up in America you'd recognize it. 'A man and a woman had a little baby, yes, they did. They had three-ee-ee in the family...' Bob signed a vinyl copy of *Multiplication Rock* for me when I was two or three years old. 'Dear Lindy,' it said, 'get big!' I hid that record, as a teenager, afraid that people would see the inscription and think, 'She took *that* a little too seriously.'

I dislike 'big' as a euphemism, maybe because it's the one chosen most often by people who mean well, who love me and are trying to be gentle with my feelings. I don't want the people who love me to avoid the reality of my body. I don't want them to feel uncomfortable with its size and shape, to tacitly endorse the idea that fat is shameful, to pretend I'm something I'm not out of deference to a system that hates me. I don't want to be gentled, like I'm something wild and alarming. (If I'm going to be wild and alarming, I'll do it on my terms.) I don't want them to think that I need a euphemism at all.

'Big' is a word we use to cajole a child: 'Be a big girl!' 'Act like the big kids!' Having it applied to you as an adult is a cloaked reminder of what people really think, of the way we infantilize and desexualize fat people. (Desexualization is just another form of sexualization. Telling fat women they're sexless is still putting women in their sexual place.) Fat people are helpless babies enslaved to their most capricious cravings. Fat people do not know what's best for them. Fat people need to be guided and scolded like children. Having that awkward, babyish word dragging on you every day of your life, from childhood into maturity, well, maybe it's no wonder that I prefer hot chocolate to whisky and substitute Harry Potter audiobooks for therapy.

Every cell in my body would rather be 'fat' than 'big'. Grown-ups speak the truth.

Please don't forget: I am my body. When my body gets smaller, it is still me. When my body gets bigger, it is still me. There is not a thin woman inside me, awaiting excavation. I am one piece. I am also not a uterus riding around in a meat incubator. There is no substantive difference between the repulsive campaign to separate women's bodies from their reproductive systems – perpetuating the lie that abortion and birth control are not healthcare – and the repulsive campaign to convince women that they and their body size are separate, alienated entities. Both say, 'Your body is not yours.' Both demand, 'Beg for your humanity.' Both insist, 'Your autonomy is conditional.' This is why fat is a feminist issue.

All my life people have told me that my body doesn't belong to me.

As a teenager, I was walking down the street in Seattle's International District, when an old woman rushed up to me and pushed a business card into my hand. The card was covered in characters I couldn't read, but at the bottom it was translated: 'WEIGHT LOSS/FAT BURN.' I tried to hand it back, 'Oh, no thank you,' but the woman gestured up and down at my body, up and down. 'Too fat,' she said. 'You call.'

In my early twenties, I was working a summer job as a cashier at an 'upscale general store and gift shop' (or, as it was known around my house, the Bourgeois Splendour

Ceramic Bird Emporium & Money Fire), when a tanned, wiry man in his sixties strode up to my cash register.

'Do you want to lose some weight?' he asked, with no introduction.

I laughed uncomfortably, hoping he'd go away: 'Ha ha, doesn't everyone? Ha ha.'

He pushed a brochure for some smoothie cleanse subscription over the counter at me. I glanced at it and pushed it back. 'Oh, no thank you.'

He pushed it toward me again, more aggressively. 'Take it. Believe me, you need it.'

'I'm not interested,' I insisted.

He glared for a moment, then said, 'So you're fine looking like that and getting the cancer?'

My ears roared. 'That's rude,' was all I could manage. I was still small then, inside. He laughed and walked out.

Over time, the knowledge that I was too big made my life smaller and smaller. I insisted that shoes and accessories were just 'my thing', because my friends didn't realize that I couldn't shop for clothes at a regular store and I was too mortified to explain it to them. I backed out of dinner plans if I remembered the restaurant had particularly narrow aisles or rickety chairs. I ordered salad even if everyone else was having fish and chips. I pretended to hate skiing because my giant men's ski pants made me look like a chimney and I was terrified my bulk would tip me off the chairlift. I stayed home as my friends went hiking, biking, sailing, climbing, diving, exploring – I was sure I couldn't keep up, and what if we got into a scrape? They couldn't boost me up a cliff or lower me down an embankment or squeeze me through a tight fissure or hoist me from the hot jaws of a bear. I never revealed a single crush, convinced that the idea of my disgusting body as a sexual being would send people – even people who loved me – into fits of projectile vomiting (or worse, pity). I didn't go swimming for a fucking decade.

As I imperceptibly rounded the corner into adulthood – fourteen, fifteen, sixteen, seventeen – I watched my friends elongate and arch into these effortless, exquisite things. I waited. I remained a stump. I wasn't jealous, exactly; I loved them, but I felt cheated.

We each get just a few years to be perfect. That's what I'd been sold. To be young and smooth and decorative and collectible. I was missing my window, I could feel it pulling at my navel (my obsessively hidden, hated navel), and I scrabbled, desperate and frantic. Deep down, in my honest places, I knew it was already gone – I had stretch marks and cellulite long before twenty – but they tell you that if you hate yourself hard enough, you can grab just a tail feather or two of perfection. Chasing perfection was your duty and your birthright, as a woman, and I would never know what it was like – this thing, this most important thing for girls.

I missed it. I failed. I wasn't a woman. You only get one life. I missed it.

There is a certain kind of woman. She is graceful. She

is slim. Yes, she would like to go kayaking with you. On her frame, angular but soft, a baggy T-shirt is coded as 'low-maintenance', not 'sloppy'; a ponytail is 'sleek,' not 'tennis ball on top of a mini-fridge'. Not only can she pull off ugly clothes, like hiking sandals, or 'boyfriend jeans', they somehow make her beauty thrum even more clearly. She is thrifted clothes from J.Crew. She can put her feet up on a chair and draw her knees to her chest. She can hold an ocean in her clavicle.

People go on and on about boobs and butts and teeny waists, but the clavicle is the true benchmark of female desirability. It is a fetish item. Without visible clavicles you might as well be a meatloaf in the sexual marketplace. And I don't mean Meatloaf the person, who has probably been laid lotsa times despite the fact that his clavicle is buried so deep as to be mere urban legend, because our culture does not have a creepy sexual fixation on the bones of meaty men.

Only women. Show us your bones, they say. If only you were nothing but bones.

Society's monomaniacal fixation on female thinness isn't a distant abstraction, something to be pulled apart by academics in women's studies classrooms or leveraged for traffic in shallow 'body-positive' listicles ('Check Out These Eleven Fat Chicks Who You Somehow Still Kind of Want to Bang – Number Seven Is Almost Like a Regular Woman!') – it is a constant, pervasive taint that warps every single woman's life. And, by extension, it is in the amniotic fluid of every major cultural shift.

Women matter. Women are half of us. When you raise every woman to believe that we are insignificant, that we are broken, that we are sick, that the only cure is starvation and restraint and smallness; when you pit women against one another, keep us shackled by shame and hunger, obsessing over our flaws rather than our power and potential; when you leverage all of that to sap our money and our time – that moves the rudder of the world. It steers humanity toward conservatism and walls and the narrow interests of men, and it keeps us adrift in waters where women's safety and humanity are secondary to men's pleasure and convenience.

I watched my friends become slender and beautiful, I watched them get picked and wear J.Crew and step into small boats without fear, but I also watched them starve and harm themselves, get lost and sink. They were picked by bad people, people who hurt them on purpose, eroded their confidence, and kept them trapped in an endless chase. The real scam is that being bones isn't enough either. The game is rigged. There is no perfection.

I listened to Howard Stern every morning in college on his eponymous nineties radio show. I loved Howard. I still do, though I had to achingly bow out as my feminism solidified. (In a certain light, feminism is just the long, slow realization that the stuff you love hates you.)

When I say I used to listen to Stern, a lot of people look at me like I said I used to eat cat meat, but what they don't understand is that *The Howard Stern Show* is on the air for hours and hours every day. Yes, there is gleeful, persistent misogyny, but the bulk of it, back when I was a daily obsessive, at least, was Howard seeking validation for his neuroses; his co-presenters Robin cackling about her runner's diarrhoea and Artie detailing the leviathan sandwich he'd eaten yesterday in a heroin stupor, then weeping over his debasement; Howard wheedling truth out of cagey celebrities like a surgeon; Howard buoying the news with supernatural comic timing; a Sagrada Familia of inside jokes and references and memories and love and people's lives willingly gutted and splayed open and dissected every day for the sake of good radio. It was magnificent entertainment. It felt like a family.

Except, for female listeners, membership in that family came at a price. Howard would do this thing (the thing, I think, that most non-listeners associate with the show) where hot chicks could turn up at the studio and he would look them over like a fucking horse vet – running his hands over their withers and flanks, inspecting their bite and the sway of their back, honking their massive horse jugs – and tell them, in intricate detail, what was wrong with their bodies. There was literally always something. If they were 8 stone, they could stand to be 7. If they were 6, gross. ('Why'd you do that to your body, sweetie?') If they were a C cup, they'd be hotter as a DD. They should stop working out so much – those legs are too muscular. Their 29-inch waist was subpar – come back when it's a 26.

Then there was me: 16 stone, 40-inch waist, no idea what bra size because I'd never bothered to buy a nice one because who would see it? Frumpy, miserable, cylindrical. The distance between my failure of a body and perfection stretched away beyond the horizon. According to Howard, even girls who were there weren't there.

If you want to be a part of this community that you love, I realized – this family that keeps you sane in a shitty, boring world, this million-dollar enterprise that you fund with your consumer clout, just as much as male listeners do – you have to participate, with a smile, in your own disintegration. You have to swallow, every day, that you are a secondary being whose worth is measured by an arbitrary, impossible standard, administered by men.

When I was twenty-two, and all I wanted was to blend in, that rejection was crushing and hopeless and lonely. Years later, when I was finally ready to stand out, the realization that the mainstream didn't want me was freeing and galvanizing. It gave me something to fight for. It taught me that women are an army.

When I look at photographs of my twenty-two-year-old self, so convinced of her own defectiveness, I see a perfectly normal girl and I think about aliens. If an alien came to earth – a gaseous orb or a polyamorous cat person or whatever – it wouldn't even be able to tell the difference between me and Angelina Jolie, let alone rank us by hotness. It'd be like, 'Uh, yeah, so those ones have the under-the-face fat sacks, and the other kind has that dangly pants nose. Fuck, these things are gross. I can't wait to get back to the omnidirectional orgy gardens of Vlaxnoid 7.'*

The 'perfect body' is a lie. I believed in it for a long time, and I let it shape my life, and shrink it – my real life, populated by my real body. Don't let fiction tell you what to do.

In the omnidirectional orgy gardens of Vlaxnoid 7, no one cares about your arm flab.

---

* This is also the rationale that I use to feel better every time there's a 'horse meat in your IKEA meatballs' scandal. Do you think an alien could tell the difference between a horse and a cow? Please.

# Are You There, Margaret? It's Me, a Person Who Is Not a Complete Freak

The first time I was informed that my natural body was gross and bad I was at a friend's house. We were eight or nine, still young enough to call it 'playing' instead of 'hanging out', and my friend looked down at my shins shining with long, iridescent blonde hairs. 'Oh,' she said with recently learned disgust, 'you don't shave your legs?' I went home and told my mom I needed a razor. I can still see her face.

'You know,' she said, equal parts pleading and guilt-tripping, 'your grandmother never shaved her legs, and I always wished I hadn't either. Her leg hair was so soft. You can't get that back.'

'Mom, it's fine,' I groaned. I'm sure I was short with her. I didn't want to be doing this either.

I was never one of those kids who couldn't wait to grow up. Childhood was a solid scam! I had these people who bought and cooked my food, washed and folded all my clothes, gave me Christmas presents, took me on trips, kept the house clean, read out loud to me until I fell asleep, found me fascinating, and spent pretty much all their time constructing a warm, loving, safe bubble around me that gave order and character to life. Now that I'm a grown-up, what do I have to show for it? Audiobooks, taxes, dirty hardwood floors, a messed-up foot, and minus a hundred dollars? A realistic ad campaign for adulthood would never sell: Do you like candy for dinner? *And plantar fasciitis?*

Childhood suited me – I was a lucky kid, and my life was simple, it was fun – so I dug in my heels as hard as I could against every portent of growing up, puberty most of all. I was still pretty weirded out from the time my babysitter let me watch *Animal House* in fourth grade, specifically the part in which a woman apparently extrudes huge wads of white tissue from her chest cavity (is that what boobs do?!); and I wasn't entirely sold on having a vagina at that point, so I sure as shit wasn't ready for it to transform into a chocolate fountain (SORRY) and turn my pants into a crime scene once a month. What a stupid thing for a vagina to do! And I had to run a terrifying pink knife all over my legs and armpits once a week to get rid of perfectly innocuous little blonde hairs that, as far as I could tell, served no purpose to begin with. Why did I grow them if I just had to scrape them off? Why have a vagina if it was just going to embarrass me?

'Puberty' was a fancy word for your genitals stabbing you in the back.

When you're a little kid, everyone talks about your period like it's going to be a party bus to WOOOOOOOOOOO! Mountain. It's all romantic metaphors about 'blossoming gardens' and 'unfurling crotch orchids', and kids buy into it because they don't know what a euphemism is because they're eleven. But it's also a profoundly secret thing – a confidence for closed-door meetings between women. Those two contradictory approaches (periods are the best! and we must never ever speak of them), made me feel like I was the only not-brainwashed one in a culty dystopian novel. 'Oh, yes, you can't imagine the joy readings in your subjectivity port when the Administration gifts you your woman's flow! SPEAKING OF THE FLOW OUT-SIDE OF THE MENARCHE BUNKER WILL RESULT IN DEACTIVATION.'

Girls in the seventies were the cultiest – they couldn't wait to get their periods and incessantly wrote books about it. 'Oh, I hope I get it today! I just have to bleed stinkily out of my vagina before that cow Francine.' The reality, of course, is that when you hit puberty you don't magically blossom into a woman – you're still the same tiny fool you were at puberty-minus-one, only now once a month hot brown blood just glops and glops out of your private area like a broken Slurpee machine. Forever. Or, at least, until you're inconceivably elderly, in an eleven-year-old's estimation. Don't worry, to deal, you just have to cork up your hole with this thing that's like a severed toe made out of cotton (and if you don't swap it out often enough, your legs fall off and you die). Or you wear a diaper. Or, if you have a super-chunky flow, you do both so you don't get stigmata on your pants in front of [hot eighth-grade boy I'm still too bashful to mention]. Also, your uterus is knives and you poop a bunch and you're hormonal and you get acne. Have fun in sixth grade, Margaret.

Personally, I couldn't handle that dark knowledge at all. So, before I hit puberty (and, let's be honest, for like fifteen years afterwards), I treated my reproductive system like it was the Nothing from *The NeverEnding Story*: 'When you look at it, it's as if you were blind.' I mean, I washed the parts and stuff, but I had no use for it – and the only thing I really knew was that it was eventually going to screw me over and ruin this sunny, golden childhood biz I had going on. More like vagin-UUUUUUUGGGHHHHHHHH.

If Google had existed when I was eleven, my search history would have looked something like this:

> *how much comes out*
> *how many cups come out*
> *how to stop period*
> *cancel your period*

> *people with no period*
> *spells to delay period*
> *magic to stop period*
> *blood magic*
> *witchcraft*
> *witches*
> *the witches*
> *roald dahl*
> *new roald dahl books*
> *free roald dahl books for kids*

(Priorities.)

My mom – probably sensing my anxiety – dragged me to a mother-daughter puberty class called Growing Up Female* – four hours on a sunny Saturday, trapped in my elementary school library talking about penises

---

* There was a part of 'Growing Up Female' where everyone was supposed to write their most embarrassing questions on little note cards and the pube instructor would answer them anonymously in front of the class. I don't remember what my question was, but I do remember that when I went up to put it in the pile, I recognized my mom's handwriting on the top card. 'Please talk about inverted nipples', it said, succinctly. In the pantheon of Worst Ways to Learn You Have One Weird Nipple, this ranks just above skywriting but just below a celebrity chef naming a dish after it (Lindy West's Great American Triple-Bangin' Weird Nip Diesel Dip). Also, it was a totally unnecessary horror, as my inverted nipple eventually became an extroverted nipple ALL ON ITS OWN. It's even considering going to some open-mic nights. Seriously, you should come.

and nipples with my mom. Strangely enough, this did not make my eventual pubin'-out process less awkward.

I don't want to give you guys TMI, but let's just say that my 'Aunt Period Blood' eventually did come to town. When it arrived, my avoidance was so finely calibrated that I blocked out the memory almost completely. I think, though I don't know for sure, that I was swimming in the ocean near my uncle's house: a wide, shallow inlet where the flats bake in the sun until the tide pours in, and then the hot mud turns the whole bay to bathwater. I can recall quick flashes of confusion and panic, guiltily unspooling toilet paper in an unfamiliar bathroom by that strange, sticky beach.

I did not want to talk about it. I avoided talking about it so assiduously that – for years – I invariably failed to tell my menopausal mom when we'd run out of stuffin' corks and diaper nuggets (#copyrighted), forcing her to run to the grocery store at inhumane hours while I squeezed out silent, single tears in the car. (If this had been a Roald Dahl book, she would have developed clairvoyance and summoned the tampons by telekinesis and/or delivery giant. Thanks for nothing, regular human mom.*)

This avoidance (and my life) reached an all-time nadir one morning when my mom didn't have time to make it to the store and back before work, so I was forced to

---

* 'Nothing' except for the unconditional love and support and meticulous care to make sure that I faced the world fully informed about my body and reproductive health! I forgive you for not being a real witch.

go to school wearing a menstrual pad belt that had been in our first aid drawer since approximately 1861. If you've never seen one of these things, because you haven't been to THE ANTIQUITIES MUSEUM, it is a literal belt that goes around your waist, with two straps that dangle down your front and back cracks, ice cold metal clips holding a small throw pillow in place over your shame canyon. I wish I could tell you I only had to go through that once before I learned my lesson.

One time, I noticed that the little waxy strips you peel off the maxi pad adhesive were printed, over and over, with a slogan: 'Kotex Understands'. In the worst moments, when my period felt like a death – the death of innocence, the death of safety, the harbinger of a world where I was too fat, too weird, too childish, too ungainly – I'd sit hunched over on the toilet and stare at that slogan, and I'd cry. Kotex understands. Somebody, somewhere, understands.*

Then, each month, once my period was over, I would burrow back into snug denial all over again: pretending my lady-parts didn't exist and that nothing would ever, ever come out of them, to the point where the blood would surprise me all over again, every month.

Twelve years later, I finally said the word 'period' out loud in public.

---

* Some forty-seven-year-old advertising copywriter in Culver City named Craig understands.

Part of that anxiety came from the fact that, particularly in my youth, I was a hider, a dissociater, a fantasist. It was easier to bury myself in stories than to deal with the fact that the realities of adulthood were barrelling down on me: money and loneliness and self-doubt and death.

Part of that anxiety came from the fact that, as a fat kid, I was already on high alert for humiliation at all times. When your body itself is treated like one big meat-blooper, you don't open yourself up to unnecessary embarrassment. I was a careful, exacting child. I hoarded my dignity. Even now, I watch where I step. I double-fact-check before I publish. I avoid canoes.

The most significant source of my adolescent period anxiety was the fact that, in America and much of the West in 2016 (and far more so in 1993), acknowledging the completely normal and mundane function of most uteruses is still taboo. The taboo is so strong that it contributes to the widespread stonewalling of women from seats of power – for fear that, as her first act in the White House, Hillary Clinton might change Presidents' Day to Brownie Batter Makes the Boo-Hoos Stop Day. The taboo is strong enough that a dude once broke up with me because a surprise period started while we were having sex and the sight of it shattered some pornified illusion he had of women as messless pleasure pillows. The taboo is so strong that while we've all seen swimming pools of blood shed in horror movies and action movies and even on the news, when a woman ran the 2015 London Marathon without a tampon, photos of blood spotting her running gear made the social media rounds to near-universal disgust. The blood is the same – the only difference is where it's coming from. The disgust is at women's natural bodies, not at blood itself.

We can mention periods obliquely, of course, when we want to delegitimize women's real concerns, dismiss their more inconvenient emotions, and perpetuate the myth that having outie junk instead of innie junk (and a male gender identity) makes a person an innately more rational and competent human being. But to suggest that having a period isn't an abomination, but is, in fact, natural and good, or – my God – to actually let people see what period blood looks like? (This is going to blow a lot of you guys' minds, but: It looks like blood.) You might as well suggest replacing the national anthem with Donald Trump harmonizing with an air horn.

Yeah, personally I hate my period and think it's annoying and gross, but it's not more gross than anything else that comes out of a human body. It's not more gross than faeces, urine, pus, bile, vomit, or the grossest bodily fluid of them all – in my mother's professional opinion – phlegm. And yet we are not horrified every time we go to the bathroom. We do not stigmatize people with stomach flu. The active ingredient in period stigma is misogyny.

This is just a wacky idea I had, but maybe it's not a coincidence that, in a country where half the population's normal reproductive functions are stigmatized,

American uterus- and vagina-havers are still fighting tooth and nail to have those same reproductive systems fully covered by the health insurance that we pay for. Maybe periods wouldn't be so frightening if we didn't refer to them as 'red tide' or 'shark week' or any other euphemism that evokes neurotoxicity or dismemberment. Maybe if we didn't perpetuate the idea that vaginas are disgusting garbage dumps, government officials wouldn't think of vagina care as literally throwing money away. Maybe if girls felt free to talk about their periods in shouts instead of whispers, as loudly in mixed company as in libraries full of moms, boys wouldn't grow up thinking that vaginas are disgusting and mysterious either. Maybe those parts would seem like things worth taking care of. Maybe women would go to the doctor more. Maybe fewer women would die of cervical and uterine cancer. Maybe everyone would have better sex. Maybe women would finally be considered fully formed human beings, instead of off-brand men with defective genitals.

Maybe I wouldn't have had to grow up feeling like a strip of wax paper was the only 'person' who understood me.

I don't remember how I got over it. Just time, I guess. I just waited. Eventually I moved from pads to tampons, and eventually I moved from tampons with applicators to the kind of tampons that you just poke up there with your finger, and eventually I was able to ask a female friend for a tampon without dying inside, and eventually

I was able to have a tampon fall out of my purse on a crowded bus and not construct an elaborate ruse to frame the woman next to me, and now I'm just a normal adult with a husband she's not afraid to send to the store for Tampax super-pluses. Ta-daaaah.

The truth is, my discomfort with my period didn't have anything to do with the thing itself (though, to any teenage girls reading this: yes, it is gross; yes, it hurts; no, it's not the end of the world; yes, sometimes it gets on your clothes; no, nobody will remember) – it was just part of the lifelong, pervasive alienation from my body that every woman absorbs to some extent. Your body is never yours. Your body is your enemy. Your body is gross. Your body is wrong. Your body is broken. Your body isn't what men like. Your body is less important than a foetus. Your body should be 'perfect' or it should be hidden.

Yeah, well, my name is Lindy West and I'm fat and I bleed out of my hole sometimes. My body is mine now. Kotex understands.

# How to Stop Being Shy in Eighteen Easy Steps

Don't trust anyone who promises you a new life. Pick-up artists, lifestyle gurus, face cream subscription-scheme evangelists, Weight Watchers coaches: These people make their living off of your failures. If their products lived up to their promise, they'd be out of a job. That doesn't make the self-help economy inherently sinister or their offerings wholly worthless – it doesn't mean you can't drop half a stone by eating Greek yogurt under the nurturing wing of a woman named Tanya, or lose your virginity thanks to the sage advice of an Uber driver in aviator goggles, or help your cousin's sister-in-law earn her February bonus while adequately moisturizing your face for $24.99 – we are all simply trying to get by, after all. It's just that, sadly, there are no magic bullets.* Real change is slow, hard, and imperceptible. It resists deconstruction.

Likewise, lives don't actually have coherent, linear story arcs, but if I had to retroactively tease one essential narrative out of mine, it'd be my transformation from a terror-stricken mouse-person to an unflappable human vuvuzela. I wasn't shy in a cute, normal way as a kid – I was a full-blown Mrs Piggle-Wiggle plant-radishes-in-my-ears-and-leave-me-in-the-care-of-an-impudent-parrot situation. I was clinically shy. Once, in the first grade at school, I peed my pants in class because I was too scared to ask the teacher if I could go to the bathroom. When the class bully noticed the puddle between my feet, I pointed at a water jug on the other side of the room and whispered that it had spilled. Just in one small, discrete pool under my chair. And also on my sock. And also the jug was filled with urine for some reason. State schools, am I right? (Pretty sure he bought it.)

Just a few decades later, here I am: the Ethel Merman of online fart disclosure. I now get yelled at and made fun of for a living – my two greatest fears rendered utterly toothless, and, even better, monetized. Women ask me: 'How did you find your voice? How can I find mine?' and

---

* Except for Lean Cuisine French Bread Pepperoni Pizza, which is an edible poem.

I desperately want to help, but the truth is, I don't know. I used to hate myself; eventually, I didn't any more. I used to be shy; eventually, I made my living by talking too much.

Every human being is a wet, gassy katamari of triumphs, traumas, scars, coping mechanisms, parental baggage, weird stuff you saw on the Internet too young, pressure from your grandma to take over the chip shop when what you really want to do is dance, and all the other fertilizer that makes a smear of DNA grow into a fully formed toxic avenger. Everyone is different, and advice is a game of chance. Why would what changed me change you? How do I know how I changed anyway? And how do you know when you're finished, when you're finally you? How do you clock that moment? Is a pupa a caterpillar or a butterfly?*

It's flattering to believe that we transform ourselves through a set of personal tangibles: Steely resolve and the gentle forbearance of a mysterious young widow who wandered in off the moor, but reality is almost always more mundane. Necessity. Luck. Boredom. Exhaustion. Time. Willpower is real, but it needs the right conditions to thrive.

I can tell you my specifics, though. I can tell you the stepping-stones that I remember along the path from quiet to loud – the moments when I died inside, and then realized that I wasn't actually dead, and then died

---

* RHETORICAL QUESTION – DON'T YOU DARE ANSWER IT.

inside a little bit less the next time, until now, when my wedding photo with the caption 'FAT AS HELL' was on the motherfucking cover of a *print newspaper* in England (where Mr Darcy could see it!!!!!!!!), and my only reaction was a self–high five.

Maybe, if you follow these steps to the letter, you'll end up here too.

## Step One: Shoplift One Bean

I was four years old, following my mother around the grocery store. She stopped near the bulk dry goods, and I stuck my hand deep into a crate of dried beans, cool and smooth. I thought the beans were cute – white with black freckles, like maybe you could plant one and grow a Dalmatian – and there were so many of them, one wouldn't be missed. When we got home, I showed my mother my prize. To my surprise, she was mad at me. It's just one bean, I said. It's not *stealing*.

'What if everyone who came to the grocery store took "just one bean"? How many beans would the grocery store have left?'

This was an incomplete story problem. How many beans were in the crate? How many people go to the grocery store? How often do they restock the beans? I was going to need some more information.

Instead, she jumped straight to the answer: *zero more beans*. If everyone took just one bean, beans would go extinct and I would tell my grandchildren about the time I ate a burrito with the same hushed reverence my dad used when talking about riding the now-extinct Los Angeles Railway from Glendale all the way to Santa Monica. Oh my God, I realized. She was going to make me RETURN THE BEAN.

We drove (*drove*! wasted fossil fuels! we fight wars over those!) back to the store. The teenager mopping the meat section looked up at us.

'Can I help you?'

'My daughter has something she'd like to tell you.'

I proffered my Dalmatian egg, rigid with terror and barely audible. 'I took this. I'm sorry.'

'Oh, uh,' he said, glancing at what was, unmistakably, just some fucking bean, 'it's okay. It's not a big deal.'

'No,' my mom corrected. 'She needs to learn.' I don't know what would constitute adequate compensation for being forcibly dragged into a small child's object lesson about accountability and theft while you were just trying to finish your blood mopping so you could make it to Amber's house party later, but $4.25 an hour wasn't it. He played along anyway.

'Oh. Um. Thanks for being honest? Don't do it again.'

'I won't,' I whispered. And I never did.*

---

* A few months ago I was at a pharmacy with my mom and walked out absentmindedly clutching a pack of antacid chews. In the parking lot I said, 'Oh!' and uncurled my fist. She looked at me like, 'You know what to do.' We went back in.

## Step Two: Accidentally Make Fun of Your Mom's Friend's Barren Womb

Eight years old. My mom's friend spread her arms for a hug: 'Come here, sweetie!' Hopped up on my latest vocab test, I gasped in mock horror, 'Are you STERILE?!'

I thought 'sterile' meant 'germ-free'. Turns out, it also means that your uterus doesn't work any more because you're old and/or the victim of some authoritarian eugenics program. She quipped something dry and perfect like, 'that I can't remember.' Everyone laughed at me and I hid in a small cupboard for one year.

## Step Three: Do a Mediocre Oral Presentation on Thelonious Monk

When you grow up with a four-hundred-year-old jazz dad instead of the three-hundred-year-old rock 'n' roll dads all your friends have, sometimes your cultural references are weird and anachronistic. For my lower-school Language Arts class, we had to do a fifteen-minute oral presentation on the black artist of our choice, and while 99 per cent of kids were like 'Whitney Houston!' or 'Denzel Washington!' I was all, 'Pioneering jazz iconoclast Thelonious Monk, a-doy.' Which is actually a pretty cool pick, in retrospect – and even at the time was not inherently embarrassing – but, nevertheless, an oral presentation violated my 'never speak audibly to anyone but my mom's leg' policy, so I spent the week leading up to the event in a shivering flop sweat.

As I sat in the back of the class, waiting for my name to be called and trying not to lose consciousness, a wave of sudden, intellectualized calm washed over me – a tipping point so unanticipated that it still feels a hair supernatural. I looked to my left at the kid who'd been carrying around a 'pet' light bulb since kindergarten. I looked to my right at the girl I'd once watched eat an entire tube of ChapStick for 'lunch dessert'. What the fuck was I scared of again? These people? It made no sense. Talking in front of people is the same as any other kind of talking, I realized – and anyway, do you know who's more intimidating than a bunch of bogey-encrusted thirteen-year-olds? MY MOM. I talked to her all the time. I could do this.

I went up and did my presentation and I wasn't scared at all and the only thing that happened was that people were bored because kids don't care about Thelonious Monk.

## Step Four: Get a Show Dog

Mozart was a Tibetan terrier, a fairly uncommon breed – too big to be hilarious but too small to be useful – designed to sit on a mountain and keep a monk company. He had long, white fur, Crohn's disease, and the personality of an Elliott Smith song. We got him when I was about 14 from a woman named Linda, with the caveat that she be allowed to continue showing and breeding him indefinitely. We were forbidden to cut his hair or tamper with his testicles. He was allergic to all common proteins, so my mom would buy whole rabbits from the butcher and cook up mounds of rabbit meat for the dog. For breakfast he had scrambled eggs.

'Hey, Mom, can I have some scrambled eggs?'

'You know how to cook. Mozart doesn't.'

At least one weekend a month, Linda would come pick up Sunwind Se-Aires Rinpoche (his show name, in case you thought I wasn't dead fucking serious) and bring him back a few days later covered in ribbons. More often than not, we'd go to the dog show too and cheer him on, and Linda would prod me to become a junior handler.* I thought about it. I really did. A couple of times I even pawed wistfully through trousersuits in the basement of the mall. But there are some lines you just can't cross.

## Step Five: Join a Choir with Uniforms that Look Like Menopausal Genie Costumes

Okay, so it was these massive palazzo pants – like polyester JNCO jeans – with a long-sleeved velour shirt, a teal cummerbund, and a felt waistcoat festooned with paisley appliqués

---

\* Have you ever been around dog show people? One time I overheard a prospective buyer talking to a basenji breeder about the breed's distinctive 'yodel'. 'They don't bark,' the breeder said, 'but they can make a noise like a woman being raped!'

and rhinestones. The overall effect was 'mother-of-the-bride at a genie wedding who hot-glue-gunned her outfit in the carparks of a Hobbycraft'.

I was in this choir for ten years.*

## Step Six: Watch *Trainspotting* with Your Parents

Contrary to all of your body's survival instincts, this is not, in fact, fatal.

## Step Seven: Read High Fantasy on the School Bus

Oh, you think you're a badass for leaving the book jacket on *Half-Blood Prince*? You think it makes you a 'total nerd' because you're trying to get through *A Clash of Kings* before the next season of *Game of Thrones* comes out? Try reading Robert Jordan on the bus in 1997 with your bass clarinet case wedged between your legs while wearing a Microsoft Bob promotional T-shirt your dad brought home from work. Then try losing your virginity.

---

* Choir actually changed my life and taught me how to dedicate myself to a collective and settle for nothing less than excellence, but, holy God, the outfits were fucked.

## Step Eight: Break a Heel on the Stairs in Your College's Humanities Building and Fall Down So Everyone Sees Your Underpants

You know what's a liberating thing to figure out? Everyone's butt looks basically how you think it looks.

## Step Nine: Taco the Back Wheel of Your Tiny Friend's Tiny Bicycle in Amsterdam

I TOLD HER IT WOULDN'T WORK.

## Step Ten: Neglect to Tell the Heavy Metal Doofus You Lose Your Virginity to that It's Your First Time and Then Bleed All Over His Bed

'Okay, but, having your bed anointed with virgin's blood is like the most metal thing ever, right?'

'You should go.'

## Step Eleven: Ignore Several Weeks of Voicemails from Your Landlord

This was back when you had to actually physically call a phone number and type in a code to retrieve your own voicemails, which means I literally never did it. Too bad I missed the heads-up that my landlord would be touring my apartment with two appraisers from the insurance company just as I stepped out of the shower fully nude and singing 'Just Around the Riverbend' from the soundtrack of Disney's *Pocahontas*! YOU'RE WELCOME FOR THE BONERS, INSURANCE APPRAISERS.

## Step Twelve: Have Sex that Is Not Silent and Still

On November 17, 2010, I received this email from my handsome, gay apartment manager:

Hi Lindy,

Sorry to have to be the bearer of this type of complaint, but it is what it is, and we're both adults.

I have had complaints from tenants regarding 'sex noise' coming from your apartment, really late at night. The complaints are about creaking and vocalizations late at night (3am).

Thanks,
[REDACTED]

Well, I am a dead body now, so problem solved.

## Step Thirteen: Tip Over a Picnic Table
## While Eating a Domino's Personal Pan
## Pizza in the Press Area of a Music Festival

A music festival is a kind of collective hangover in which people who are cooler than you compete to win a special kind of lanyard so they can get into a special tent with unlimited free snacks. The only food available to the non-lanyarded hoi polloi is expensive garbage dispensed resentfully from a shack, which is how I found myself, in 2010, sitting alone at a picnic table in the press area of the Sasquatch! Music Festival, sweatily consuming a $45 Domino's pepperoni personal pan pizza and a Diet Pepsi and hoping nobody noticed me.

Someone was interviewing the band YACHT at the next table, and I was sort of dispassionately staring at my phone, pretending like my friends were texting me even though they weren't because I think they were all back in the free snacks area playing VIP four-square with Adele or something probably. I watched the woman from YACHT do her interview for a few minutes before I remembered that we'd gone to college together, where, even before experimental pop fame, she'd been an untouchably cool and talented human lanyard who was also beautiful and nice. I chewed my oily pork puck.

A little gust of wind picked up and blew my Domino's napkin off the picnic table and on to the ground.

No big deal. I leaned over, nonchalantly, to pick it up. Gotta have a napkin! Can't be a fat lady eating pizza with red pig-grease all over my face! Unfortunately, due to my intense preoccupation with not drawing attention to myself while eating a Domino's personal pepperoni pan pizza in public at a music festival while fat, I misjudged the flimsy plastic picnic table's centre of gravity.

When I leaned over to grab the napkin, the table leaned over too.

I fell in the dirt. The pizza fell on top of me. The Diet Pepsi tipped over and glugged out all over my dress. The table fell on top of the Pepsi on top of the pizza on top of me. The napkin fluttered away. EVERYONE LOOKED AT ME. The music journalists looked at me. The band YACHT looked at me. In an attempt at damage control, I yelled, 'I'm really drunk, so it's okay!' which wasn't even true, but apparently it's better to be drunk at ten in the morning than it is to be a human being who weighs something? All that anxiety about trying not to be a gross, gluttonous fat lady eating a 'bad' food in public, and I wound up being the fat lady who was so excited about pizza that she threw herself to the ground and rolled around in it like a dog with a raccoon carcass. Nailed it.

## Step Fourteen: Get Hired to Write a Press Release for the Band Spoon, Then Write

Something So Weird and Unusable that the Band Spoon Quietly Sends You a Cheque and Never Speaks to You Again and Hires Someone Normal to Write a Real Press Release

Here is the actual full text that I actually emailed to Britt Daniel of the band Spoon:

> *Some years ago in the past (no one knows how many for sure), a baby was born: his mother's pride, hearty and fat, with eyes like pearls and fists like very small fingered hams. That baby was named David Coverdale of Whitesnake. Meanwhile, on the other side of the world and many, many years later, an even better and newer baby came out. They called that one Britt Daniel of Spoon. The two would never meet.*
>
> *The son of an itinerant barber-surgeon (his motto: 'Oops!') and his raven-haired bride who may or may not have been Cher (she definitely wasn't, say 'historians'), Daniel spent his formative years traversing America's heartland, on leech duty in the back of the amputation/perm wagon. Despite mounting pressure to join the family business – 'the Daniel child's bonesaw work truly is a poem!' swooned* Itinerant Barber-Surgeon's Evening Standard Digest *– Daniel heard the siren song of song-singing and fled the narrow confines of his itchy-necked, blood-spattered world.*

*Little is known of Daniel's whereabouts and associations in these dark interim years (when consulted for comment, David Coverdale of Whitesnake said, 'Get away from me, please'), but he emerged in 1994, saw his shadow, and formed the band Spoon, stronger and taller and more full of handsome indie rock and roll than ever before. After the great big success of 2001's* Girls Can Tell, *2002's* Kill the Moonlight, *2005's* Gimme Fiction, *and 2007's* Ga Ga Ga Ga Ga, *Daniel – along with Jim Eno (inventor of the bee beard), Eric Harvey (feral child success story), and Rob Pope (white male) – birthed* Transference: *in Daniel's words, Spoon's 'orangest' and 'most for stoners' album yet.*

*Asked about her son's new record, Daniel's mother, who is definitely 'not' Cher, quipped: 'Too metal!' Reached for comment on whether or not Daniel's non-Cher mother is really qualified to judge the metalness of things, David Coverdale of Whitesnake said, 'Seriously, how did you get this number?'*

I am so, so sorry, the band Spoon.

## Step Fifteen: Get a Job Blogging for a National Publication with Thousands and Thousands of Commenters Who Will Never Be Satisfied No Matter What You Write

At a certain point you just have to be like [jack-off motion] and do you.

## Step Sixteen: Ask Acclaimed Journalist Pat Mitchell if She Is Actress Marlo Thomas at a Banquet Honouring Acclaimed Journalist Pat Mitchell

Hollyweird Fun Fact: Pat Mitchell does not like this at all.

## Step Seventeen: Break a Chair While Sitting on the Stage at a Comedy Show

I went to see my friend Hari work out some new jokes at a small black-box theatre in Seattle. The ancient theatre seats were too narrow for my modern butt, so I moved to an old wooden chair that had been placed on the side of the stage as overflow seating. A few minutes into Hari's set, a loud crack echoed through the theatre and I felt the chair begin to collapse under me. I jumped into a kind of emergency squat, which I nonchalantly held until the producer rushed out from backstage and replaced my chair with some sort of steel-reinforced military-grade hydraulic jack.

## Step Eighteen: Admit that You Lied Earlier About How Old You Were When You Peed Your Pants in Class

Third grade. I was 8 years old, okay? Are you happy?

This is the only advice I can offer. Each time something like this happens, take a breath and ask yourself, honestly:

Am I dead? Did I die? Is the world different? Has my soul splintered into a thousand shards and scattered to the winds? I think you'll find, in nearly every case, that you are fine. Life rolls on. No one cares. Very few things – apart from death and crime – have real, irreversible stakes, and when something with real stakes happens, humiliation is the least of your worries.

You gather yourself up, and you pick the pepperoni out of your hair, and you say, 'I'm sorry, Pat Mitchell, it was very nice to meet you,' and you live, little soldier. You go live.

# When Life Gives You Lemons

I don't keep track of my periods and kind of think anyone who does is some sort of neuroscientist, so I have no idea what prompted me to walk over to Walgreens pharmacy and buy a pregnancy test. Maybe women really do have a weird, spiritual red phone to our magic triangles. I never thought I did, but for whatever reason, that day, I walked around the corner, bought the thing, took it home to my studio apartment, and peed on it. I probably bought some candy and toilet paper too as, like, a decoy, so maybe the Walgreens cashier would think the pregnancy test was just a wacky impulse buy on my way to my nightly ritual of wolfing Mars bars while taking a magnum dump.

I always throw a decoy purch' in the cart any time I have to buy something embarrassing like ice cream or vagina plugs. (Obviously, on paper, I disagree with this entire premise – food and hygiene are not 'embarrassing' – but being a not-baby is a journey, not a destination.) Like, if I want to eat six lollipops and a frozen pizza for dinner, I'll also buy a lemon and a bag of baby carrots to show that I am a virtuous and cosmopolitan duchess who just needs to keep her pantry stocked with party pizza in case any Ninja Turtles stop by. The carrots are for me, Belvedere. Or, if I want to buy the super-economy box of ultra-plus tampons, I'll also snag a thing of Windex and some sandwich meat, to distract the cashier from the community theatre adaptation of *Carrie* currently entering its third act in my gusset. Maybe I'm just buying these tampons for my neighbour on my way to slam some wafer-thin turkey and polish my miniatures, bro! (IMPORTANT: One must NEVER EVER use tampons and Ben & Jerry's as each other's decoy purchases, as this suggests you are some sort of Bridget Jones situation who needs ice cweam to soothe her menses a-bloo-bloos, which defeats the entire purpose of decoy purchases, Albert Einstein.)

So, peeing on things is weird, right? As a person without a penis, I mean. I could show you the pee-hole on any crotch diagram – I could diagram pee-holes all day (AND I DO) – but in practice, I'm just not…entirely clear on where the pee comes out? It's, sort of, the front area? The foyer? But it's not like there's, like, a nozzle. Trying to pee into a cup is like trying to fill a beer bottle with a Super Soaker from across the room in the dark. On a moonless night. (This is one of those disheartening moments where I'm realizing that I might be The Only One, and I may as well have just announced to you all that I don't know how shoes work. What's the deal with these hard socks??? Right, guys?

. . .

. . . .

. . . Guys?)

So, I pee on the thing a little bit, and on my hand a lot, and these two little pink lines appear in the line box. The first line is like, 'Congratulations, it's urine', and the second line is like, 'Congratulations, there's a baby in it!'

This was not at all what I was expecting and also exactly what I was expecting.

My 'boyfriend' at the time (let's call him Mike) was an emotionally withholding, conventionally attractive jock whose sole metric for expressing affection was the number of hours he spent sitting platonically next to me in coffee shops and bars without ever, ever touching me. To be fair, by that metric he liked me a lot. Despite having nearly nothing in common (his top interests included cross-country running, fantasy cross-country running [he invented it], New England the place, New England the idea, and going outside on Saint Patrick's Day; mine were candy, naps, hugging, and wizards), we spent a staggering amount of time together – I suppose because we were both lonely and smart, and, on my part, because he was the first human I'd ever met who was interested in touching my butt without keeping me sequestered in a mouldy basement, and I was going to hold this relationship together if it killed me.

Mike had only been in 'official' relationships with thin women, but all his friends teased him for perpetually hooking up with fat chicks. Every few months he would get wasted and hold my hand, or tell me I was beautiful, and the first time I tried to leave him, he followed me home and said he loved me, weeping, on my doorstep. The next day, I told him I loved him too, and it was true for both of us, probably, but it was a shallow, watery love – born of repetition and resignation. It condensed on us like dew, only because we waited long enough. But 'I have grown accustomed to you because I have no one else' is not the same as 'Please tell me more about your thoughts on the upcoming New England colleges cross-country season, my king'.

It was no kind of relationship, but, at age twenty-seven, it was still the best relationship I'd ever had, so I set my jaw and attempted to sculpt myself into the kind of golem who was fascinated by the 10k finishing times of someone who still called me his 'friend' when he talked to his mom. It wasn't fair to him either – he was clear about his parameters from the beginning (he pretty much told me: 'I am emotionally withdrawn and can only offer you two to three big spoons per annum'), but I pressed myself against those parameters and strained and pushed until he and I were both exhausted. I thought, at the time, that love was perseverance.

I'm not sure how I got pregnant – we were careful, mostly – but, I don't know, sometimes people just fuck up. I honestly don't remember. Life is life. If I had carried that pregnancy to term and made a half-Mike/half-me human baby, we may have been bound to each other forever, but we would have split up long before the birth. Some people should not be together, and once the stakes are real and kicking and pressing down on your bladder, you can't just pretend shit's fine any more. Mike made me feel lonely, and being alone with another person is much worse than being alone all by yourself.

I imagine he would have softened, and loved the baby; we would share custody amicably; maybe I'd move into my parents' basement (it's nice!) and get a job writing technical case studies at Microsoft, my side gig at the time; maybe he'd just throw child support at me and move away, but I doubt it. He was a good guy. It could have been a good life.

He didn't want to be in Seattle, though – New England pulled at his guts like a tractor beam. It was all he talked about: flying down running trails at peak foliage; flirting with Amherst college girls in Brattleboro bars; keeping one foot always on base, in his glory days, when he was happy and thrumming with potential. He wanted to get back there. Though it hurt me at the time (why wasn't I as good as running around in circles in Vermont and sharing growlers of IPA with girls named Blair?!), I wanted that for him too.

As for me, I found out I was pregnant with the part-Mike foetus just three months before I figured out how to stop hating my body for good, five months before I got my first email from a fat girl saying my writing had saved her life, six months before I fell in love with my future husband, eight months before I met my stepdaughters, a year before I moved to Los Angeles to see what the world had for me, eighteen months before I started working at *Jezebel*, three years before the first time I went on television, four years and ten months before I got married to the best person I've ever met, and just over five years before I turned in this book manuscript.

Everything happened in those five years after my abortion. I became myself. Not by chance, or because an abortion is some mysterious, empowering feminist bloode-magick rite of passage (as many, many – *too many for a movement ostensibly comprising grown-ups* – anti-choicers have accused me of believing), but simply because it was time. A whole bunch of changes – set into motion years, even decades, back – all came together at once, like the tumblers in a lock clicking into place: my body, my work, my voice, my confidence, my power, my determination to demand a life as potent, vibrant, public, and complex as any man's. My abortion wasn't intrinsically significant, but it was my first big grown-up decision – the first time I asserted, unequivocally, 'I know the life that I want and this isn't it'; the moment I stopped being a passenger in my own body and grabbed the rudder.

So, I peed on the thingy and those little pink lines showed up all, 'LOL hope u have $600, u fertile betch', and I sat down on my bed and I didn't cry and I said, 'Okay, so this is the part of my life when this happens.' I didn't tell Mike; I'm not sure why. I have the faintest whiff of a memory that I thought he would be mad at me. Like getting pregnant was my fault – as though my clinginess, my desperate need to be loved, my insistence that we were a 'real' couple and not two acquaintances who had grown kind of used to each other, had finally congealed into a hopeful, delusional little bundle and sunk its roots into my uterine wall. A physical manifestation of how pathetic I was. How could I have let that happen? It was so embarrassing. I couldn't tell him. I always felt alone in the relationship anyway; it made sense that I would deal with this alone too.

It didn't occur to me, at the time, that there was anything complicated about obtaining an abortion. This is a trapping of privilege: I grew up middle-class and white in Seattle, I had always had insurance, and, besides, abortion was legal. So, I did what I always did when I needed a common, legal, routine medical procedure – I made an appointment to see my doctor, the same doctor I'd had since I was twelve. She would get this whole implanted embryo mix-up sorted out.

The nurse called my name, showed me in, weighed

me, tutted about it, took my blood pressure, looked surprised (fat people can have normal blood, NANCY), and told me to sit on the paper. I waited. My doctor came in. She's older than me, with dark, tightly curled hair, motherly without being overly familiar. 'I think I'm pregnant,' I said. 'Do you want to be pregnant?' she said. 'No,' I said. 'Well, pee in this cup,' she said. I peed all over my hand again. 'You're pregnant,' she said. I nodded, feeling nothing.

I remember being real proud of my chill 'tude in that moment. I was the Fonz of getting abortions. 'So, what's the game plan, Doc?' I asked, popping the collar of my leather jacket like somebody who probably skateboarded here. 'Why don't you go ahead and slip me that RU-486 prescriptsch and I'll just [moonwalks toward exam room door while playing the saxophone].'

She stared at me.

'What?' I said, one hundred combs clattering to the floor.

Turns out, THE DOCTOR IS NOT WHERE YOU GET AN ABORTION.

I'd been so sure I could get this taken care of today, handle it today, on my own, and move on with my life – go back to pretending like I had my shit together and my relationship was bearable, even good. Like I was a normal woman that normal men loved. When she told me I had to make an appointment at a different clinic, which probably didn't have any openings for a couple of weeks, and started writing down phone numbers on a Post-it, I crumpled.

'That's stupid,' I sobbed, my anxiety getting the better of me. 'You're a doctor. This is a doctor's office. Do you not know how to do it?'

'I covered it in medical school, yes,' she said, looking concerned in an annoyingly kind way, 'but we don't do them here at this clinic.'

'Well, why did I even come here, then? Why didn't they tell me on the phone that this appointment was pointless?'

'You want reception to tell everyone who calls in that we don't do abortions here, no matter what they're calling about?'

'YES,' I yelled.

She didn't say anything. I heaved and cried a little bit more, then a little bit less, in the silence.

'Is there anything else I can do for you right now?' she asked, gently.

'No, I'm fine.' I accepted a tissue. 'I'm sorry I got upset.'

'It's okay. This is a stressful situation. I know.' She squeezed my shoulder.

I went home, curled up in bed, and called the clinic (which had some vague, mauve, nighttime soap name like 'Avalon' or 'Dynasty' or 'Falcon Crest'), still wobbling on the edge of hysteria. Not for all the reasons the forced-birth fanatics would like you to think: not because my choice was morally torturous, or because I was ashamed, or because I couldn't stop thinking about the tiny fingernails of our 'baby', but because life is fucking hard, man. I wanted someone to love me so much. I did want a baby, eventually. But what I really wanted was a family. Mike wasn't my family. Everything was wrong. I was alone and I was sad and it was just hard.

The woman on the phone told me they could fit me in the following week, and it would be $400 after insurance. It was the beginning of the month, so I had just paid rent. I had about $100 left in my bank account. Payday was in two weeks.

'Can you bill me?' I asked.

'No, we require full payment the day of procedure,' she said, brusque from routine but not unkind.

I felt like a stripped wire. My head buzzed and my eyes welled.

'But...I don't have that.'

'We can push back the appointment if you need more time to get your funds together,' she offered.

'But,' I said, finally breaking, 'I can't be pregnant any more. I need to not be pregnant. I'm not supposed to be pregnant.'

I didn't want to wait two more weeks. I didn't want to think about this every day. I didn't want to feel my body change. I didn't want to carry and feed this artefact of my inherent unlovability – this physical proof that any permanent connection to me must be an accident. Men made wanted babies with beautiful women. Men made mistakes with fat chicks. I sobbed so hard I think she was terrified. I sobbed so hard she went to get her boss.

The head of the clinic picked up the phone. She talked to me in a calm, competent voice – like an important businesswoman who is also your mom, which is probably fairly accurate. She talked to me until I started breathing again. She didn't have to. She must have been so busy, and I was wasting her time with my tantrum. Babies having babies.

'We never do this,' she sighed, 'because typically, once the procedure is done, people don't come back. But if you promise me you'll pay your bill – if you really promise – you can come in next week and we can bill you after the procedure.'

I promised, I promised, I promised so hard. Yes, oh my God, yes. Thank you so much. Thank you. Thank you! (And I did pay – as soon as my next paycheck came in. They were so surprised, they sent me a thank-you card.)

I like to think the woman who ran the clinic would have done that for anyone – that there's a quiet web of women like her (like us, I flatter myself), stretching from pole to pole, ready to give other women a hand. She helped me even though she didn't have to, and I am forever grateful. But I also wonder what made me sound, to her ears, like someone worth trusting, someone it was safe to take a chance on. I certainly wasn't the neediest person calling her clinic. The fact is, I was getting that abortion no matter what. All I had to do was wait two weeks, or have an awkward conversation I did not want to have with my supportive, liberal, well-to-do mother. Privilege means that it's easy for white women to do each other favours. Privilege means that those of us who need it the least often get the most help.

I don't remember much about the appointment itself. I went in, filled out some stuff on a clipboard, and waited to be called. I remember the waiting room was crowded. Everyone else had somebody with them; none of us made eye contact. I recognized the woman working the front desk – we went to high school together (which should be illegal)* – but she didn't say anything. Maybe that's protocol at the vagina clinic, I thought. Or maybe I just wasn't that memorable as a teenager. Goddammit.

Before we got down to business, I had to talk to a counsellor, I guess to make sure I wasn't just looking for one of those cavalier partybortions that the religious right is always getting its sackcloth in a bunch over. (Even though, by the way, those are legal too.) She was younger than me, and sweet. She asked me why I hadn't told my 'partner', and I cried because he wasn't a partner at all and I still didn't know why I hadn't told him. Everything after that is vague. I think there was a blood test and maybe an ultrasound. The doctor, a brisk, reassuring woman with grey hair in an almost military buzz cut, told me my

---

* Same goes for you, dildo store cashier. (But thank you for the discount.)

embryo was about three weeks old, like a tadpole. Then she gave me two pills in a little cardboard wallet and told me to come back in two weeks. The accompanying pamphlet warned that, after I took the second pill, chunks 'the size of lemons' might come out. LEMONS. Imagine if we, as a culture, actually talked frankly and openly about abortion. Imagine if people seeking abortions didn't have to be blindsided by the possibility of blood lemons falling out of their vaginas via a pink photocopied flyer. Imagine.

That night, after taking my first pill, as my tadpole detached from the uterine wall, I had to go give a film-making prize to my friend and colleague Charles Mudede – make a speech on a stage in front of everyone I knew, at the Genius Awards, the *Stranger*'s annual arts grant. It was surreal. Mike and I went together. We had fun – one of our best nights. There are pictures. I'm glassy-eyed, smiling too big, running on fumes and gallows humour. I remember pulling a friend into a dark corner and confessing that I had an abortion that day. 'Did they tell you the thing about the lemons?' she asked. I nodded. 'Don't worry,' she whispered, hugging me tight. 'There aren't going to be lemons.'

She paused.

'Probably no lemons.'

Afterwards, Mike didn't want to stay over at my place because he had to get up early to go to his high school reunion. That was fine. (It wasn't.) I've got some uterine lining to shed, bozo. I tried to drop him off Fonz-style, but he could tell I was being weird. It's hard to keep secrets from people you love, even when your love isn't that great.

'What's going on?' he said, as we sat in my quietly humming Volvo in the alley behind his house.

'I can't tell you,' I said, starting to cry.

There was silence, for a minute.

'Did you have an abortion?' he said.

'Today,' I said.

He cried too – not out of regret or some moral crisis, but because I'd felt like I had to keep this a secret from him. We were just so bad at being together. He felt as guilty as I felt pathetic, and it made us closer, for a while.

He still went to his reunion the next day, and he didn't text enough, and I cried a little. I lay in bed all day and ached. No lemons came out. It was like a bad period. The day after that, I felt a little better, and the day after that was almost normal. I wasn't pregnant any more. But instead of going back to our old routine – him running, me chasing – something had shifted inside me. Within six months, we were broken up for good. Within seven months, I wasn't mad at him any more. Within a year, he moved back east. He was a good guy.

I hesitate to tell this story, not because I regret my abortion or I buy into the right-wing narrative that pregnancy is God's punishment for disobedient women, but because it's so easy for an explanation to sound like a justification. The truth is that I don't give a damn why anyone has an abortion. I believe unconditionally in the right of people with uteruses to decide what grows inside of their body and feeds on their blood and endangers their life and reroutes their future. There are no 'good' abortions and 'bad' abortions, there are only pregnant people who want them and pregnant people who don't, pregnant people who have access and support and pregnant people who face institutional roadblocks and lies.

For that reason, we simply must talk about it. The fact that abortion is still a taboo subject means that opponents of abortion get to define it however suits them best. They can cast those of us who have had abortions as callous monstrosities, and seed fear in anyone who might need one by insisting that the procedure is always traumatic, always painful, always an impossible decision. Well, we're not, and it's not. The truth is that life is unfathomably complex, and every abortion story is as unique as the person who lives it. Some are traumatic, some are even regretted, but plenty are like mine.

Paradoxically, one of the primary reasons I am so determined to tell my abortion story is that my abortion simply wasn't that interesting. If it weren't for the zealous high school youth-groupers and repulsive, birth-obsessed pastors flooding the public discourse with mangled foetus photos and crocodile tears – and, more significantly, trying to strip reproductive rights away from our country's most vulnerable communities – I would never think about my abortion at all. It was, more than anything else, mundane: a medical procedure that made my life better, like the time I had oral surgery because my wisdom tooth went evil-dead and murdered the tooth next to it. Or when a sinus infection left me with a buildup of earwax so I had to pour stool softener into my ear and have an otolaryngologist suck it out with a tiny vacuum, during which he told me that I had 'slender ear canals', which I found flattering. (Call me, Dr Yang!)

It was like those, but also not like those. It was a big deal, and it wasn't. My abortion was a normal medical procedure that got tangled up in my bad relationship, my internalized fatphobia, my fear of adulthood, my discomfort with talking about sex; and one that, because of our culture's obsession with punishing female sexuality and shackling women to the nursery and the kitchen, I was socialized to approach with shame and describe only in whispers. But the procedure itself was the easiest part. Not being able to have one would have been the real trauma.

# You're So Brave for Wearing Clothes and Not Hating Yourself!

Probably the question I get most often (aside from 'Why won't you go on Joe Rogan's comedy podcast to debate why rape is bad with five amateur martial arts fighters in a small closet?') is 'Where do you get your confidence?'

'Where do you get your confidence?' is a complex, dangerous question. First of all, if you are a thin person, please do not go around asking fat people where they got their confidence in the same tone you'd ask a shark how it learned to breathe air and manage a Burger King.

As a woman, my body is scrutinized, policed, and treated as a public commodity. As a fat woman, my body is also lampooned, openly reviled, and associated with moral and intellectual failure. My body limits my job prospects, access to medical care and fair trials, and – the one thing Hollywood movies and Internet trolls most agree on – my ability to be loved. So the subtext, when a thin person asks a fat person, 'Where do you get your confidence?' is, 'You must be some sort of alien because if I looked like you, I would definitely throw myself into the sea.' I'm not saying there's no graceful way to commiserate about self-image and body hate across size-privilege lines – solidarity with other women is one of my drugs of choice – but please tread lightly.

Second of all, to actually answer the question, my relationship with my own confidence has always been strange. I am profoundly grateful to say that I have never felt inherently worthless. Any self-esteem issues I've had were externally applied – people *told me* I was ugly, revolting, shameful, unacceptably large. The world around me simply insisted on it, no matter what my gut said. I used to describe it as 'reverse body dysmorphia': When I looked in the mirror, I could never understand what was supposedly so disgusting. I knew I was smart, funny, talented, social, kind – why wasn't that enough? By all the metrics I cared about, I was a home run.

So my reaction to my own fatness manifested outwardly instead of inwardly – as resentment, anger, a feeling of deep injustice, of being cheated. I wasn't intrinsically without value, I was just doomed to live in a culture that hated me. For me, the process of embodying confidence was less about convincing myself of my own worth and more about rejecting and unlearning what society had hammered into me.

Honestly, this 'Where do you get your confidence?' chapter could be sixteen words long. Because there was really only one step to my body acceptance: Look at pictures of fat women on the Internet until they don't make you uncomfortable any more. That was the entire process. (Optional step two: Wear a crop top until you forget you're wearing a crop top. Suddenly, a crop top is just a top. Repeat.)

It took me a while to put my foot on that step, though. So let me back up.

The first time I ever called myself fat, in conversation with another person, was in my second year of college. My roommate, Beth – with whom I had that kind of platonically infatuated, resplendent, despairing, borderline codependent friendship unique to young women – had finally convinced me to tell her who I had a crush on, and didn't understand why the admission came with a Nile of tears. I couldn't bear to answer her out loud, so we IMed in silence from opposite corners of our dorm room. 'You don't understand,' I wrote, gulping. 'You count.'

Beth is one of those bright, brilliant lodestones who pulls people into her orbit with a seemingly supernatural inevitability. She wore high heels to class, she was a salsa dancer and a soprano, she could change the oil in a truck and field dress a deer, she got Distinction on our English exams even though she and I only started studying two days before (I merely passed), and she could take your hands and stare into your face and make you feel like you were the only person in the world. It seems like I spent half my college life wrangling the queue of desperate, weeping suitors who'd 'never felt like this before', who were convinced (with zero input from her) that Beth was *the one*.

She regularly received anonymous flower deliveries: tumbling bouquets of yellow roses and trailing greens, with rhapsodic love letters attached. She once mentioned, offhand on the quad, that she wanted one of those Leatherman multi-tools, and a few days later one appeared, sans note, in her campus mailbox. In retrospect, these years were a nonstop, fucked-up carnivale of male entitlement (the anonymous Leatherman was particularly creepy, the subtext being 'I'm watching you'), one young man after another endowing Beth with whatever cocktail of magic dream-girl qualities he was sure would 'complete' him, and labouring under the old lie that wearing a girl down is 'seduction'. At the time, though, we laughed it off. Meanwhile, alone in my bed at night, the certainty that I was failing as a woman pressed down on me like a quilt.

I was the girl kids would point to on the playground and say, 'She's your girlfriend', to gross out the boys. No one had ever sent me flowers, or asked me on a date, or written me a love letter (Beth literally had 'a box' where she 'kept them'), or professed their shallow, impetuous love for me, or flirted with me, or held my hand, or bought me a drink, or kissed me (except for that dude at that party in freshman year who was basically an indiscriminate roving tongue), or invited me to participate in any of the myriad romantic rites of passage that I'd always been told were part of normal teenage development. No one had *ever picked me*. Literally no one. The cumulative result was worse than loneliness: I felt unnatural. Broken. It wasn't fair.

'You will always be worth more than me, no matter what I do,' I told Beth, furious tears splashing on my Formica desk. 'I will always be alone. I'm fat. I'm not stupid. I know how the world works.'

'Oh, no,' she said. 'I wish you could see yourself the way I see you.'

I resented her certainty; I thought she didn't understand. But she was just ahead of me.

The first time I ever wrote a fat-positive sentence in the newspaper (or said a fat-positive sentence out loud, really) was four years later, in December 2006 in my review of the movie *Dreamgirls* for the *Stranger*:

'I realize that Jennifer Hudson is kind of a superchunk, but you kind of don't mind looking at her, and that kind of makes you feel good about yourself. But...fat people don't need your pity.'

It was early enough in my career (and before the Internet was just a 24/7 intrusion machine) that my readers hadn't yet sniffed out what I looked like, and coming this close to self-identifying as fat left me chattering with anxiety all day. My editor knew what I looked like. Would she notice I was fat now? Would we have to have a talk where she gave me sad eyes and squeezed my arm and smiled sympathetically about my 'problem'? Because I *just said* fat people don't need your pity.

Of course she never mentioned it. I don't know if she even picked up on it – if she turned my body over in her head as she read that sentence. She probably didn't. I didn't know it at the time, but the idea of 'coming out' as fat comes up a lot in fat-acceptance circles. I always thought that if I just never, ever acknowledged it – never wore a bathing suit, never objected to a fat joke on TV, stuck to 'flattering' clothes, never said the word 'fat' out loud – then maybe people wouldn't notice. Maybe I could pass as thin, or at least obedient. But, I was slowly learning, you can't advocate for yourself if you won't admit what you are.

At the same time, I was blazingly proud that I'd stuck that sentiment in my *Dreamgirls* review – right there in the opening paragraph, where it couldn't be missed. It was exhilarating to finally express something (even in the most oblique way possible) that I'd been desperately hiding for so long. From a rhetorical standpoint, it tidily expressed a few complex concepts at once: Fat people are not here as a foil to boost your own self-esteem. Fat people are not your inspiration porn. Fat people can be competent, beautiful, talented, and proud without your approval.

Not a ton had changed in my self-conception since that conversation with Beth. I had finally found someone to flirt and have sex with, but he wouldn't be seen on the street with me or call me his girlfriend. He also believed in the Sasquatch, wore a T-shirt that said, 'I'm the drunken Irishman your mother warned you about', and eventually dumped me for someone irritatingly named Mindy. We then had a screaming fight, which culminated in him attempting to 'slam' the door in my face with a flourish, except he lived in a dank basement accessed via a garage and could only emphatically push the garage door button and stand there glaring as it '*whirrrrrrrrrrrrrrrrrrrrrr*'ed to the ground in slow motion. My cab-driver hit on me while I sobbed, and a small voice inside reminded me I should be flattered.

Lots of men wanted to have sex with me – I dated casually, I got texts in the night – they just didn't want to go to a restaurant with me, or bring me to their office party, or open Christmas presents with me. It would have been relatively simple to swallow the idea that I was objectively sexually undesirable, but the truth was more painful: There was something about me that was *symbolically shameful*. It's not that men didn't like me; it's that they hated themselves for doing so. But why?

The question, 'Why am I like this?' gnawed at me.

The media tells me that I'm fat because a weird sandwich exists somewhere with Krispy Kreme doughnuts instead of bread. But I'm sure that's not it. I would definitely remember eating that sandwich. Internet trolls tell me I'm fat because I eat lard out of a bucket for dinner, which would be a weird thing to do, and use a Toblerone for a dildo, which really isn't an efficient way to ingest calories at all. The fact is that I'm fat because life is a snarl of physical, emotional, and cultural forces both in and out of my control. I'm fat because life is life.

Like most fat people who've been lectured about diet and exercise since childhood, I actually know an inordinate amount about nutrition and fitness. The number of nutrition classes and hospital-sponsored weight loss programs and individual dietician consultations and tear-filled therapy sessions I've poured money into over the years makes me grind my teeth. (Do you know how many Jet Skis I could have bought with that money? *One Jet Skis!!!*) I can rattle off how many calories are in a banana or an egg or six almonds or a Lean Cuisine Santa Fe-Style Rice and Beans ready-meal. I know the difference between spelt bread and Ezekiel bread, and I know that lemon juice makes a great 'sauce'! I could teach you the proper form for squats and lunges and kettle-bell swings, if you want. I can diagnose your shin splints. I can correct your jump shot.

I never did manage to lose weight, though – not significantly – and my minor 'successes' weren't through any eating patterns that could be considered 'normal'. The level of restriction that I was told, by professionals, was necessary for me to 'fix' my body essentially precluded any semblance of joyous, fulfilling human life.

It was about learning to live with hunger – with feeling 'light', I remember my nutritionist calling it – or filling your body with chia seeds and this miracle supplement that expanded into a bulky viscous gel in your stomach. If you absolutely had to have food in between breakfast at seven a.m. and lunch at one p.m., try six almonds,* and if you've already had your daily almond allotment, try an apple. So crisp. So filling. Then everyone in nutrition class would nod about how fresh and satisfying it is to just eat an apple.

One day, during the Apple Appreciation Circle-Jerk Jamboree, the only other fat person in the class (literally everyone else was an affluent suburban mom trying to lose her last four pounds of baby weight) raised his hand and mentioned, sheepishly, that he sometimes felt nauseated after eating an apple, a weird phenomenon I was struggling with as well. What was that all about? Was there any way to fix it? The nutritionist told us she'd recently read a study about how some enzyme in apples caused nausea in people with some *other* elevated enzyme that became elevated when a person was fat for a long time. So, basically, if we fatties wanted to be able to eat

---

* 'Six almonds.' – All diet advice.

apples again, nausea-free, then we'd really need to double down on the only-eating-apples diet. The only real cure for fatness was to go back in time and not get fat in the first place. I started to cry and then I started to laugh. What the fuck kind of a life was this?

Around that time, just when I needed it, Leonard Nimoy's *Full Body Project* came to me like a gift. The photographs are in black and white, and they feature a group of fat, naked women laughing, smiling, embracing, gazing fearlessly into the camera. In one, they sway indolently like the Three Graces; in another they re-create photographer Herb Ritts's iconic pile of supermodels. It was the first time I'd ever seen fat women presented without scorn.

I clicked, I skimmed, I shrugged, I clicked away.

I clicked back.

I was ragingly uncomfortable. *Don't they know those things are supposed to stay hidden?* I haven't been having basement sex with the lights off all these years so you could go show what our belly buttons look like!

At the same time, I felt something start to unclench deep inside me. What if my body didn't have to be a secret? What if I was wrong all along – what if this was all a magic trick, and I could just *decide I was valuable* and it would be true? Why, instead, had I left that decision in the hands of strangers who hated me? Denying people access to value is an incredibly insidious form of emotional violence, one that our culture wields aggressively and liberally to keep marginalized groups small and quiet. What if you could opt out of the game altogether? I paused and considered. When the nutrition teacher emailed, I didn't sign up for the next session of Almond Gulag.

I couldn't stop looking. It was literally the first time in my life that I'd seen bodies like mine honoured instead of lampooned, presented with dignity instead of scorn, displayed as objects of beauty instead of as punch lines. It was such a simple manoeuvre, but so profound. Nimoy said, of his models, 'I asked them to be proud.' For the first time it struck me that it was possible to be proud of my body, not just in spite of it. Not only that, but my bigness is powerful.

I hate being fat. I hate the way people look at me, or don't. I hate being a joke; I hate the disorienting limbo between too visible and invisible; I hate the way that complete strangers waste my life out of supposed concern for my death. I hate knowing that if I did die of a condition that correlates with weight, a certain subset of people would feel their prejudices validated, and some would outright celebrate.

I also love being fat. The breadth of my shoulders makes me feel safe. I am unassailable. I intimidate. I am a polar icebreaker. I walk and climb and lift things, I can open your jar, I can absorb blows – literal and metaphorical – meant for other women, smaller women, breakable women, women who need me. My bones feel like iron – heavy, but strong. I used to say that being fat in our culture was like drowning (in hate, in blame, in your own tissue), but lately I think it's more like burning. After three decades in the fire, my iron bones are steel.

Maybe you are thin. You hiked that trail and you are fit and beautiful and wanted and I am so proud of you, I am so in awe of your wiry brightness; and I'm miles behind you, my breathing ragged. But you didn't carry this up the mountain. You only carried yourself. How hard would you breathe if you had to carry me? You couldn't. But I can.

I was hooked. Late at night, I started furtively clicking through fat-positive tags on Tumblr like a Mormon teen looking at Internet porn. Studies have shown that visual exposure to certain body types actually changes people's perception of those bodies – in other words, looking at pictures of fat people makes you like fat people more. (Eternal reminder: Representation matters.)

I discovered a photo blog called '*Hey, Fat Chick*' (now, crushingly, defunct) run by an effervescent Australian angel named Frances Lockie, and pored over it nightly like a jeweller or a surgeon or a codebreaker. It was pure, unburdened joy, and so simple: Just fat women – some bigger than me, some smaller – wearing outfits and doing things and smiling. Having lives. That's it. They were like medicine. One by one they loosened my knots.

First, I stopped reacting with knee-jerk embarrass-ment at the brazenness of their bodies, the way I'd been trained. I stopped feeling obscene, exposed, like someone had ripped the veil off my worst secrets.

Next, they became ordinary. Mundane. Neutral. Their thick thighs and sagging bellies were just bodies, like any other. Their lives were just lives, like any other. Like mine.

Then, one day, they were beautiful. I wanted to look and be like them – I wanted to spill out of a crop top; plant a flag in a mountain of lingerie; alienate small, bitter men who dared to presume that women exist for their consumption; lay bare the cowardice in recoiling at something as *literally fundamental* as a woman's real body. I wasn't unnatural after all; the cultural attitude that taught me so was the real abomination. My body, I realized, was an opportunity. It was political. It moved the world just by existing. What a gift.

# The Red Tent

In August of 2010, when I was writing for the *Stranger*, Seattle's alternative weekly newspaper, we got an email from an organization called 'Vashon Red Tent', advertising that 'A Red Tent Temple Sisterhood Is Coming to Vashon.' Vashon is an island, accessible by ferry from Seattle, mainly populated by NIMBY-ish hippies, NIMBY-ish yuppies, boutique farmers, and wizards riding recumbent bicycles. A full quarter of the children in Vashon schools are unvaccinated. The 'Red Tent Temple Movement', the press release read, 'envisions a gathering honouring our stories and promoting healing in every town across the country where women of all ages meet regularly to support one another and their monthly menstrual cycles'.

The only thing I knew about Anita Diamant's novel *The Red Tent*, which inspired the movement, was that one time my college roommate read it and then announced to the rest of us that she wanted to go 'bleed into the forest'. It didn't feel like a good sign. This event, clearly, was my worst nightmare. The paper, clearly, RSVPed for me immediately.

I dragged my friend Jenny along with me, and we barely made the ferry. On the bench next to us there was a woman with long frizzy hair and high-waisted jeans. She was wearing a T-shirt with a picture of cats in sunglasses playing saxophones, and above the picture it said, 'JAZZ CATS'. 'There are a lot of different ways to be a woman,' I wrote in my notebook. Jenny and I were running late for menses tent, but we stopped by the grocery store anyway to buy some boxed wine and anxiety jelly beans. We sat in the parking lot and wolfed beans and got as tipsy as we could in the time allotted.

My sister is into this sort of thing. She loves ritual. She's forever collecting shells for her Venus altar, or tying a piece of ribbon to a twig in a secret grove, or scooping magic waters up into very small vials to make potions. Being around my sister feels magical. When we travelled through Europe together (following the path of Mary Magdalene, doyeeeee), we didn't miss a stone circle or a magic well – tromping over stiles and up tors and always leaving little offerings for the fairies. Once, in Cornwall, we looked down into an aquamarine cove and she said, 'Do you see the mermaids? They're sitting on that rock.' I said no, and she looked at me with pity. On the way to the Vashon Red Tent Temple, I texted my sister for advice. 'I'm on my way to a new moon celebration at a menses temple,' I said. 'Liar,' she said. 'It's true! Any tips?' 'Stay open to a new flow and wave goodbye to the blood of old that nurtured you well.' I knew she'd know what to do.

I almost didn't go in. It was too intimate and foreign, and I am clinical like my mom. I like magic *as escapism* – I barely tolerate fantasy books set in our universe (the first time I cracked a Harry Potter novel I was like, 'Yo, is this a documentary?') – pretending that the supernatural is real just drives home how much it's not. But we did, we walked in, removed our shoes, and joined the circle of women seated on pillows beneath the homemade canopy of red scarves. It wasn't really a 'tent' so much as a pillow fort inside a community centre, but it did the job.

The women were talking about chocolate, which was such an adorable cliché that I fell in love with them instantly. 'There is *definitely* a goddess of chocolate.' 'I read somewhere that the molecular makeup of chocolate is so unique that it was probably brought here from another planet.' One woman passed a Hershey's bar around the circle. 'This chocolate is even better now that it's passed through the hands of so many goddesses,' said the woman next to me, appreciatively.

There was chanting.

Isla, the leader of the circle, said that right now there is an astrological configuration – the Cardinal Cross – that has not occurred since Jesus was alive, and that she and the other local angel healers are very busy 'holding that energy'. She explained that the media tells us that things are terrible and violent, but that this is actually one of the most peaceful times in history. We should not focus on the negative. Later, I asked my sister what an 'angel healer' is, and she said, 'Well, you know, angels are just the same thing as aliens. They're probably the ones who brought the chocolate.' I asked about the Cardinal Cross, and she told me, 'If you're going to have a baby, have it like tomorrow. It'll be a superbaby. Dude, remind me to send you a picture of the cosmos right now. It's fucking out of control.'

We went around the circle and stated our 'intentions' for the coming moon cycle. Most of the women had intentions that I didn't understand, that involved 'manifesting' and 'balance' and 'rhythm'. One woman said that her intention was to 'end rape'. I said I intended to organize my apartment, and felt mundane. The women totally approved. Total approval is the point of menses tent. The press release had promised 'a place where young women can ask questions and find mentors in absolute acceptance', and menses tent delivered.

'You look different today,' said one woman to another. 'Oh, I know,' she replied. 'It's because I did the twenty-four-strand DNA activation yesterday. I feel like a completely new person.' The women around me tittered with excitement. I asked what that meant. She explained that in addition to our two physical DNA strands, we have twenty-two spiritual DNA strands, which can be 'activated' by a specially trained lady with a crystal wand.

The process took ten hours. 'There's also a golden gate that you can walk through,' she said, 'but that's more for larger groups.' Then another woman explained that DNA activation has something to do with the Mayan calendar. I still didn't understand. My sister didn't know anything about DNA activation, but she did tell me a story about the time she went to see a shaman and the shaman had a spirit jaguar eat a ghost off her back. That sounded cooler than the DNA thing.

Jenny and I thanked our hostesses and hobbled out to the car, thighs asleep and buzzing with pain after hours of sitting cross-legged on pillows. We ate some more jelly beans and talked about our feelings.

It's true that I don't believe in most of this stuff – and I suspect that believing is the secret ingredient that makes this stuff work. But it *does* work for the gracious ladies on the pillows under the red tent, and it was surprisingly nurturing to sit cross-legged in their world for a few hours. And even though I would never phrase it like this, I agree that women don't always get a chance to 'fill our own vessels'. My dad worked all day. My mom worked all day, then came home and made dinner. Women do a lot. Women are neat.

Back at the office, I knew my job was to make fun of menses tent, but I just didn't want to. They were so nice and so earnest. What was the point of hurting them? Sincerity is an easy target, but I don't want to excise sincerity from my life – that's a lonely way to live.

I used to try to be cool. I said things that I didn't believe about other people, and celebrities, and myself; I wrote mean jokes for cheap, 'edgy' laughs; I neglected good friendships for shallow ones; I insisted I wasn't a feminist; I nodded along with casual misogyny in hopes that shitty dudes would like me.

I thought I was immune to its woo-woo power, but if it hadn't been for menses tent, how long would it have taken me to understand that I get to choose what kind of person to be? Open or closed? Generous or cruel? Spirit jaguar or clinging ghost? A lazy writer (it's easy to hate things) or a versatile one? I don't believe in an afterlife. We live and then we stop living. We exist and then we stop existing. That means I only get one chance to do a good job. I want to do a good job.

# Hello, I Am Fat

In 2009, I'd been at the *Stranger* about five years (four as a freelancer, one on staff), and was casually dating a dude who refused to kiss me on the mouth. He's a good person; he was good to me in other ways. They all were, really – even Sasquatch garage door guy – but, you know, we were all raised in the same fucking septic tank. No one teaches young men how to take care of fat girls.

The *Stranger* is the best thing that's ever happened to me. I got to learn how to write and run a newspaper from geniuses (David Schmader, Charles Mudede, Eli Sanders) I'd been obsessed with since I was a teen – we took chances, changed elections, ran our sections with nearly unfettered editorial freedom, and struck a balance between ethics and irreverence that I was always proud of. By the time I got on staff full-time, Dan Savage was already medium-famous and had orchestrated a more-power/less-responsibility promotion from editor in chief to editorial director, so he wasn't in the office so much. Nonetheless, the culture of the place was all Dan, and even mostly in absentia he did the hell out of that job.

Dan would run a meeting every few weeks, always our most productive and most boisterous; be gone travelling for months and then show up at a candidate interview to grill local politicians with the acuity of a day-to-day city hall reporter; emerge from his office like a groundhog to drop an infuriatingly brilliant mandate about precisely how to tweak whatever delicate story was stumping us; and send insistent emails the morning after every office party to ensure surplus sheet cake was placed, uncovered, on his desk. (Dan has a thing about stale cake.) I was taught a mantra, my first week, to manage my expectations about Dan as an editor: 'Silence is praise.' As long as you don't know he exists, you're killing it. I remember two editors improvising an extensive, Dan-themed Gilbert and Sullivan musical number over their cubicle walls: 'I will laugh at you when you cry!' Dan, the great and terrible.

If his management approach is unique, Dan's editorial sense – for clear-headed satire and gleeful, pointed disobedience, for where to aim and from what angle to drop the hammer – is unparalleled in my decade of writing experience. Dan knows how to land a point better than anyone I've ever worked with. That preternatural ability is what has made him famous (he is a magnificent pundit), and it's also what gets him into trouble.

Like all of us, Dan fucks up. Like all of us, he is some-times slow to find the right side of an issue. And when he has an opinion on something, he expresses it in vivid, uncompromising prose to a rapt audience of millions – over and over and over again, because he is as prolific as he is stubborn. He also, like all of us, can be intract-able and defensive when criticized, and because he is very funny and very smart, he can also be very snide, and when such a person does actually happen to be wrong, but mistakes totally warranted criticism for petty sniping, and responds not with openness but with sneering acidity to a critic who is just trying to advocate for their own humanity, it can be a very bad look.

This is the great curse of popularity and the great luxury of obscurity: People only care about your mistakes when they can hear you. Only failures can afford to be cavalier and careless.

Unfortunately for my personal emotional cankers, in the mid-to-late noughties Dan was on something of an 'obesity epidemic' kick. He wasn't alone. At the same time that I was tentatively opening to the idea that my human-ity was not hostage to my BMI, the rest of the nation had declared a 'war on obesity'. They'd whipped up a host of reasons why it was right and good to hate fat people: our repulsive, unsexy bodies, of course (the classic!), but also our drain on the healthcare system, our hogging of plane armrests, our impact on 'the children', our pathetic inabil-ity and/or monstrous refusal to swap austerity for gluttony (like thin people, who, as you know, are moderate and virtuous in all ways). Oh, and our 'health'. Because they care. They abuse us for our own good. (Do you know what is actually not a good way to help a group of people, it turns out? Advocating for their eradication.)

Dan was on that train, and I don't blame him – it was a very popular (and, I imagine, gratifying) ticket at the time, and, even more so than today, it was considered very roguish to 'tell it like it is' about fat people (as though that wasn't the status quo, as though we hadn't got the message). I understand; I had only recently snapped out of some of the same thought patterns myself. I had to learn how to look at pictures of fat people, and I am one.

The problem is, fat people are an extremely suboptimal bogeyman, the roots of America's 'obesity epidemic' lying largely in systemic poverty and agribusiness, not in those exploited thereby; the problems with America's fucked-up healthcare system stemming entirely from America's preposterous healthcare system, not from the people attempting to survive within it (and use a service they pay tremendous amounts of money for); new research finding that it's a sedentary lifestyle, not size, that correlates with increased health risks; and fat people turning out to *be people* whose lives are impossibly complex snarls of external and internal forces and who do not, in fact, owe you shit. As Kate Harding and Marianne Kirby wrote in their book *Lessons from the Fat-O-Sphere*, health is not a moral imperative.

However, it is easier to mock and deride individual fat people than to fix food, desserts, school lunches, corn subsidies, inadequate or nonexistent public transportation, unsafe sidewalks and parks, healthcare, mental healthcare, the minimum wage and your own insecurities. So, 'personal responsibility' was de rigueur, and my boss was on board.

It was the same bunk you were hearing everywhere around that time – imperious declarations about fat people's delusions and gluttony, soaked in plausible deniability about 'health'. Dan's main sticking point seemed to be fat people (like me) who insisted we weren't imminently dying – he fiercely and persistently defended his 'refusal to take the self-esteem-boosting/public-health-shredding position that you can be obese and healthy'.

In one 2004 column, the root of a whole pantload of his fatphobia accusations, Dan got grumpy about women, 'particularly obese people', wearing low-rise jeans, and dismissed the impact that stigmatizing language has on young women:

'It's an article of faith that we can't talk about how much crap we're eating – or how awful we look in low-rise jeans – without inducing eating disorders in millions of silly and suggestible young women... Our obsession with anorexia... not only covers up America's true eating disorder (we eat too much and we're too fat!), but it also hamstrings efforts to combat obesity, a condition that kills almost as many people every year as smoking does. Eating disorders, by way of comparison, lead to only a handful of deaths every year. If you're truly concerned about the health and well-being of young women...worry more about the skyrocketing rates of obesity-related diseases in young people – like type 2 diabetes – and less about the imaginary link between anorexia and my low opinion of low-rise jeans.'

Okay, man. We get it. You are not into those jeans.

More than anything, though, this passage from his 2005 book *The Commitment* sums up the overall tone of his stance, at the time, on fatties:

> 'Two days later, in a water park in Sioux Falls, South Dakota, I came to a couple of realizations: First, any-one who denies the existence of the obesity epidemic in the United States hasn't been to a water park in Sioux Falls, South Dakota. (The owners of water parks in the U.S. must be saving a fortune on water and chlorine bills; floating in the deep end of the wave pool with D.J., Terry observed that there was an awful lot of water being displaced. If the South Dakotans floating around us all got out of the pool at the same time, the water level would most likely have dropped six feet.)'

We are horrible to look at, we are in the way, we are a joke.

I could probably have dealt with that – after all, it really was coming from all sides – but in an unanticipated side effect, a few perspicacious trolls made the connection between my fat body and Dan's fatphobia. (Comments sections on any post about fatness were their own kind of horror – having my workplace host sentiments such as 'I wouldn't fuck with these people. They might sit on you and crush you to death. If they can catch you, of course. Best bet: run uphill, you'll induce a heart attack, and the pursuer might even roll back downhill, taking out the other members of the fat mob' didn't exactly make me feel supported.)

I started to get comments here and there, asking how it felt to know that my boss hated me because of my body. I knew Dan didn't hate me – we had always gotten along, he made me a writer, and sometimes I even earned the vocal kind of praise! – but if that was true, why didn't he give this thing a rest? Why didn't he see that when he wrote about fat people, he was writing about me, Lindy West, his colleague and friend? Why should I, as an employee, have to swallow that kind of treatment at my job – in the same newspaper I was sweating blood into for $36k a year? What's more, what about our fat readers? I knew there were people reading the blog, clocking the fact that I wasn't sticking up for them – as though I was tacitly okay with what Dan was arguing. It implied complicity and self-hatred. Did I want to be the kind of person who didn't fight?

Crop tops, short shorts, no kissing on the mouth, the *whirrrrrrrrrrrrr* of the garage door, Beth's flowers, my perfect blood pressure, the trolls, a year in a basement talking about fucking Sasquatch ('I don't know why they don't just find out what it eats and then go to where that is!'), all of it, a lifetime of it, finally foamed up and spilled over. Something lurched awake inside of me. They talk to you this way until you 'come out' as fat. They talk to you this way until you make them stop.

I emailed Dan, privately, in November of 2009. In my memory, I asked him to please, please consider his words more carefully before writing about fat people – to remember that we are human beings with complex lives, not disease vectors or animals. I begged him to extend some compassion to the fat people on his staff, and to imagine what it might feel like to read your boss parroting the same cruel words and snide insinuations that have been used to hurt you and hold you back your whole life. I was timid, pleading.

Or, at least, that's how I remember it.

While writing this chapter, I looked up the original exchange, and it turns out that my memory sucks. Here's the actual email that I sent to my actual boss:

*To: Dan Savage*
**Subject:** *'Hello! Could you lay off the fat people shit?'*

*Just curious: Who are these hordes of fat people chasing you around insisting that eating pot pies all day is awesome and good for your health? Because, um, I don't believe you. That sounds like a straw man, and I*

*know 'some of your best friends are fat' or whatever, but*
*you sound like a bigot. Also, your (super fucking obvious*
*and regressive) point has been made – everyone in the*
*world already thinks fat people are lazy and gross! WE*
*GET IT. YOU ARE NOT BREAKING NEW GROUND*
*HERE.*

*And just so you know, on top of the trolls who call*
*me a fat cunty virgin every day of my life, now I also*
*get trolls asking me, 'How does it feel to know your*
*boss thinks you're a disgusting cow?' Being fat is its*
*own punishment. I don't give a shit if you think I lie*
*on the couch all day under the Dorito funnel – I'd just*
*rather not be abused on the Internet from inside my own*
*workplace. Just a thought.*

*Love,*
*Lindy*

Ohhhhh, past self. You are completely nanners. (I
mean, let's be honest. I was really popular. I knew they
wouldn't fire me.)

Dan's reply was nine words long. He asked, simply, if
I'd ever detected any animus from him personally.

'Nope, not at all,' I wrote. 'Not my point at all, either.'

He said he heard me, but I was accusing him of being
a bigot – a serious charge against someone exhibiting, by
my admission, no animus.

It was a dodge. He was deliberately missing the point.

## SO THEN I REALLY WENT FOR IT:

*Sorry I hurt your feelings?*

*My points again: Being fat is its own punishment. Every day. Fat people know they're fat and that the rest of the world thinks they're disgusting. Have you experienced pop culture recently? You are crusading for a stereotype that is already the majority opinion. Why bother? Why is that interesting? There is no army of fat acceptance warriors poised to overthrow the earth and force-feed you gravy. Don't worry – all the stereotypes about fat people are solidly intact.*

*I'm being sincere here. I don't really think you're a bigot – I just think you're acting like one. This is a really painful thing that I wake up with every morning and go to sleep with every night, AND I'M NOT EVEN THAT FAT.*

Dan never wrote back. We never talked about it in the office.

He couldn't really be mad, could he? The whole ethos of the *Stranger* – an ethos that Dan built – was editorial freedom, thoughtful provocation, and fearless transparency. Dan taught me to be bold and uncompromising, to confront bullshit head-on, to cultivate a powerful voice and use it to effect meaningful change. I learned it from watching you, Dan. *I learned it from watching you.*

For the next year, he went back to posting semi-regularly about the horrors of the obesity epidemic with no discernible interruption, and I went back to ignoring him. Then, a whole lot happened in the same week. I dumped no-kissing-on-the-mouth guy. I kissed (on the mouth!) the man who, four years later, would become my husband. Then, Dan wrote a *Slog* post entitled, 'Ban Fat Marriage', using the supposed health risks of fatness as leverage to skewer some Republican dodo's argument that gay marriage should be illegal because gay people supposedly die younger:

'Even if it were true – even if gay people had lower life expectancies (which we do not) – and if that "fact" all by itself was a justification for banning same-sex marriage, why stop with gay people? Iowa should ban fat marriage. There are, according to the state of Iowa, more than 1.4 million obese people living in Iowa. That's nearly 30% of the state's population, and those numbers just keep rising. The social costs of Iowa's obesity epidemic are pretty staggering – and those costs include premature death and lower average life expectancies for Iowans.'

I get the point. I understand that, in context, Dan presents 'ban fat marriage' as an instructive absurdity. This post is still dehumanizing. It still oversimplifies the connections between size and health, and, unfortunately, some anti-fat bigots actually have suggested that fat people shouldn't be allowed to have families (because of 'the children'). Mainly, though, if you have a track record of treating my struggle with persistent disrespect and dismissal, then my struggle is not yours to use as a flippant thought experiment.

I threw up a quick *Slog* post:

*Re: Ban Fat Marriage*

*Hey, Dan – so now that you're equating the stigmatization of fat people with the stigmatization of gay people, does that mean you're going to stop stigmatizing fat people on this blog?*

Nothing. I waited a few days. Nothing.

I looked back over our old email exchange – remembering how scary it had been to send, how roundly he'd dismissed me, and how quickly he'd gone back to posting fatphobic rhetoric. Passively attempting to earn my humanity by being smart, nice, friendly, and good at my job had gotten me nowhere; my private confrontation with Dan had gotten me nowhere; literally telling him 'this harms me' had gotten me nowhere; taking a quick, vague swipe at him on the blog had gotten me nowhere. So I did what – honestly – I thought Dan would do: On Feb 11, 2011, I wrote a scorched-earth essay and, vibrating with adrenaline, posted it publicly at the tail end of a sunny Friday afternoon.

The post was called, 'Hello, I Am Fat'. It included a

full-body photo of me, taken that day by Kelly O, our staff photographer, with the caption: '28 years old, female, 5'9", 263 lbs'. Remember that, at this point in my life, I had never self-identified as 'fat' except in that single email exchange with Dan, and in private conversations with trusted friends. Even then, I spoke the word only with shame, not power. Never in public. Never defiantly. Something had snapped in me the week of this post. This was a big deal, a spasm of self-determination rendered in real time. This was the moment.

It read as follows (now with a few annotations and cuts for brevity):

*This is my body (over there – see it?). I have lived in this body my whole life. I have wanted to change this body my whole life. I have never wanted anything as much as I have wanted a new body. I am aware every day that other people find my body disgusting. I always thought that some day – when I finally stop failing – I will become smaller, and when I become smaller literally everything will get better (I've heard It Gets Better)! My life can begin! I will get the clothes that I want, the job that I want, the love that I want. It will be great! Think how great it will be to buy some jeans or whatever at J.Crew. Oh, man. J.Crew. Instead, my body stays the same.*

*There is not a fat person on earth who hasn't lived this way. Clearly this is a TERRIBLE WAY TO EXIST.*

*Also, strangely enough, it did not cause me to become thin. So I do not believe any of it any more, because fuck it very much.*

*This is my body. It is MINE. I am not ashamed of it in any way. In fact, I love everything about it. Men find it attractive. Clothes look awesome on it. My brain rides around in it all day and comes up with funny jokes. Also, I don't have to justify its awesomeness/attractiveness/healthiness/usefulness to anyone, because it is MINE. Not yours.\**

*I'm not going to spend a bunch of time blogging about fat acceptance here, because other writers have already done it much more eloquently, thoroughly, and radically than I ever could. But I do feel obligated to try to explain what this all means.*

*I get that you think you're actually helping people and society by contributing to the fucking Alp of shame that crushes every fat person every day of their lives — the same shame that makes it a radical act for me to post a picture of my body and tell you how much it weighs.*

---

\* I've noticed that a lot of people have trouble with the basic definition of fat acceptance – they want to argue and nitpick about calories and cardio and insurance and health and on and on and on – and if you're one of those people, wallowing in confusion, fret no more. I can sum it up for you in one easy-to-remember phrase: GET THE FUCK OFF ME, YOU FUCKING WEIRDO. Print it, laminate it, be it.

*But you're not helping. Shame doesn't work. Diets don't work.\* Shame is a tool of oppression, not change.*

*Fat people already are ashamed. It's taken care of. No further manpower needed on the shame front, thx. I am not concerned with whether or not fat people can change their bodies through self-discipline and 'choices.' Pretty much all of them have tried already. A couple of them have succeeded. Whatever. My question is, what if they try and try and try and still fail? What if they are still fat? What if they are fat forever? What do you do with them then? Do you really want millions of teenage girls to feel like they're trapped in unsightly lard prisons that are ruining their lives, and on top of that it's because of their own moral failure, and on top of that they are ruining America with the terribly expensive diabetes that*

---

\* Fatphobes love to hold this assertion up as evidence of how delusional and intractable fat activists are. 'Calories in/calories out,' they say. 'Ever heard of thermodynamics?' 'Uhhh, I've never seen a fat person in a concentration camp. High-five, Trevor.' Leaving aside the barbarism of suggesting, however obliquely, that, well, at least concentration camp victims weren't fat, no fat activist who says 'Diets don't work' is suggesting that you cannot starve a fat person to a thin death. Rather, we are referencing the rigorously vetted academic conclusion that traditional diets – the kind that are foisted upon fat people as penance and cure-alls and our entry exam for humanity – fail 95 per cent of the time. Whether fat people fail to lose weight due to simple laziness and moral torpor or because of a more complex web of personal, cultural, and medical factors, those numbers are still real. Those fat people still exist. Pushing diet culture as a 'cure' for fatness does nothing but perpetuate the emotional and economic exploitation of fat people.

*they don't even have yet? You know what's shameful? A complete lack of empathy.*

*And if you really claim to still be confused – 'Nu uh! I never said anything u guyz srsly!' – there can be no misunderstanding shit like this:*

*'I am thoroughly annoyed at having my tame statements of fact – being heavy is a health risk; rolls of exposed flesh are unsightly – characterized as "hate speech."'*

*Ha!*

*1. 'Rolls of exposed flesh are unsightly' is in no way a 'tame statement of fact'. It is not a fact at all – it is an incredibly cruel, subjective opinion that reinforces destructive, paternalistic, oppressive beauty ideals.\* I am not unsightly. No one deserves to be told that they're unsightly. But this is what's behind this entire thing – it's not about 'health', it's about 'eeeewwwww'. You think fat people are icky. Eeeewww, a fat person might touch you on a plane. With their fat! Eeeeewww! Coincidentally, that's the same feeling that drives anti-gay bigots, no matter what excuses they drum up about*

---

\* In his response to this post, Dan took me to task for cherry-picking that quote, explaining that he wasn't mocking the flesh rolls of fat people specifically, he was mocking the flesh rolls of all women who wear low-rise jeans without having the correct bodies for it. Oh, okay. FYI, feminism isn't super jazzed about men policing women's clothing choices either. (Also, it was totally about fat people.)

'family values' and, yes, 'health'. It's all 'eeeewwwww'. And sorry, I reject your eeeeeewwww.

2. You are not concerned about my health. Because if you were concerned about my health, you would also be concerned about my mental health, which has spent the past twenty-eight years being slowly eroded by statements like the above. Also, you don't know anything about my health. You do happen to be the boss of me, but you are not the doctor of me. You have no idea what I eat, how much I exercise, what my blood pressure is, or whether or not I'm going to get diabetes. Not that any of that matters, because it is entirely none of your business.

3. 'But but but my insurance premiums!!!!' Bullshit. You live in a society with other people. I don't have kids, but I pay taxes that fund schools. The idea that we can somehow escape affecting each other is deeply conservative. Barbarous, even. Is that really what you're going for? Good old-fashioned American individualism? Please.

4. But most importantly: I reject this entire framework. I don't give a shit what causes anyone's fatness. It's irrelevant and it's none of my business. I am not making excuses, because I have nothing to excuse. I reject the notion that thinness is the goal, that thin = better – that I am an unfinished thing and that my life can really start when I lose weight. That then I will be

*a real person and have finally succeeded as a woman. I am not going to waste another second of my life thinking about this. I don't want to have another fucking conversation with another fucking woman about what she's eating or not eating or regrets eating or pretends to not regret eating to mask the regret. OOPS I JUST YAWNED TO DEATH.*

*If you really want change to happen, if you really want to 'help' fat people, you need to understand that shaming an already-shamed population is, well, shameful. Do you know what happened as soon as I rejected all this shit and fell in unconditional luuuuurve with my entire body? I started losing weight. Immediately. WELL LA DEE FUCKING DA.\**

The post went up. I left the office early and went across the street to get a head start on our Friday afternoon ritual, 'Ham Grab', so named because it consisted of getting drunk as fast as possible and then descending upon a meat and cheese platter like a plague of locusts with journalism

---

\* If I had it to do over again, I would write this last part more clearly, because I think the way it stands undermines my point a bit. What I was trying to convey was that if anti-fat crusaders really want what they claim to want – for fat people to be 'healthy' – they should be on the front lines of size acceptance and fat empowerment. There's hard science to back this up: Shame contributes measurably to weight gain, not weight loss. Loving yourself is not antithetical to health, it is intrinsic to health. You can't take good care of a thing you hate.

degrees. As the comment section churned away – two hundred, three hundred, four hundred comments – I heard nothing from Dan all weekend; unbeknownst to me, he was off the grid in a cabin somewhere with no mobile or Internet service. It would be a jarring welcome back to civilization. Oops.

The following Monday, Dan posted his response. It was three times longer than my piece – 2,931 words, to be exact – accused me of 'ad hominem attacks' and being blinded by my own emotional problems, and featured, as its centerpiece, this condescending bit of armchair psychology:

> *It sounds like you're externalizing an internal conflict about being fat – you're projecting your anger and self-loathing on to me, and seeing malice and bigotry where none exists, and perhaps that's useful because that anger seems to be liberating and motivating. If having your own personal boogeyman on Slog helps you conquer your shame and love your body and this helps you break out of old, self-destructive patterns and habits (you can't be losing weight now just because your attitude changed), then I'm happy to be your own personal boogeyman. But honestly, Lindy, you don't need one. You're stronger than that.*

He said a lot of other things too, like 'the bigotry in my posts exists only in Lindy's imagination', and 'there are crazy fat people out there, Lindy…be careful who you crawl into bed [with] now that you're a "brave" hero to the FA movement', and approvingly quoted a commenter who suggested that 'apparently, Lindy isn't very good with reading comprehension'.

It was exhausting – it just felt so static and pointless. We hadn't moved an inch. The next day, there was a staff meeting about how I'd hurt Dan's feelings, with no mention at all of the climate that had led me to write the post in the first place. I was livid. I thought about quitting, but the *Stranger* meant everything to me – it was the place where I found my voice, and the family that emboldened me to use it. At the time, I couldn't imagine anything beyond that office, and besides, I loved working for Dan.

So, I dropped the argument (I'd said my piece, I stood by it, and a lot of people agreed) and we fell back into a normal routine. Gotta get the paper out. Meanwhile, I started getting emails from fat people, both friends and strangers, telling me that my post had made their lives better in small ways – emboldened them to set a boundary of their own, or take in their reflection with care rather than disgust. To this day, those emails make my job worth it.

A few weeks later, Dan and I went out for beer and soft pretzels to make sure we were cool.

'It's like,' I said, 'here we are at this restaurant. Say both of our chairs are broken.'

'Okay,' said Dan.

'If my chair collapses under me right now, people will assume it's because I'm fat. But if your chair collapses under you, it's because you sat on a broken chair.'

'Okay.'

'Do you get it?'

'I get it.'

I never wanted an apology, I just wanted it to be different. And, after all that, it was. While writing this chapter, when I went back and read Dan's response for the first time in years, I was shocked at how dated it feels. The Dan I know in 2016 – I don't see much of him there. Whether I had anything to do with it or not, he writes about fat people differently now. When someone asks him for advice about body image, he reaches out to a fat person (sometimes me) for input. When fat people would make an easy punch line, he doesn't take it.

We, as a culture, discuss fat people differently now too. If you go back to just 2011, 2010, 2009 – let alone 2004 or 2005, when Dan was writing about the Sioux Falls water park and low-rise jeans – the rhetoric, even on mainstream news sites, was vicious. Vicious was normal. It was perfectly acceptable to mock fat bodies, flatten fat humanity, scold fat people for their own deaths. You only have to look back five years to see a different world, and, by extension, tangible proof that culture is ours to shape, if we try.

Obviously there's no shortage of fat-haters roaming the Internet, the beach, and America's airports in 2016, but an idea has taken root in the hive mind: We do not speak about human beings this way.

I tell this story not to criticize Dan, but to praise him. Change is hard, and slow, but he bothered to do it. Sometimes people on the defensive rebound into compassion. Sometimes smart, good people are just a little behind.

# Why Fat Lady So Mean to Baby Men?

I'm on hold with the FBI. I clack out an email to a customer service rep at MailChimp, simultaneously filling out boilerplate help-desk forms for Twitter, Google, and Yahoo. Intermittently, I refresh my email and skim through hundreds and hundreds of spam letters ('Confirm your subscription for Subscribe2 HTML Plugin', 'European Ombudsman Newsletter', 'Potwierdzenie prenumeraty newsletter tvp.pl'), tweezing out legitimate messages from my agent, my editors, my family. I know I'm missing things. I'm probably losing money.

When the emails started trickling into my inbox that morning, I'd thought little of it. Some days are spammier than others. Around ten a.m., the trickle swelled to a flood, and then a creepy tweet popped up too: 'Email me at [toiletperson@thetoilet.net] if you want the spam to stop. I simply want you to delete an old tweet.'

I sigh, scrubbing my face hard with a dry palm. Does this have to be today? I was going to write about my abortion today!

The receptionist from the Seattle FBI office picks up.

'Hi,' I say. 'I have...a problem?' I'm already grasping for words. How do you explain to someone who might not even know what Twitter is that you're being anonymously extorted via email newsletters into deleting an unspecified past tweet? Beyond that, how do you convince them that it actually matters? My understanding of the FBI is 90 per cent *X-Files*. As far as I know, they're off trying to solve Sasquatch crime, and here I am begging them for tech support.

It does matter, though. It's costing me time, potential income, and mental health. If you consider Twitter part of my work, which I do, it is tampering with a journalist's email to coerce them into pulling a story. It is, I think, illegal. More significantly, though, it's part of a massive, multifarious online harassment campaign that has saturated my life for the past half decade – and, on a broader scale, is actively driving women off the Internet. Disruption, abuse, the violent theft of time, then writing about it to illuminate what we go through online – this is my whole deal now. Unsurprisingly, the tweet that [the toilet] wanted deleted turned out to be a screenshot of a rape threat I'd received from a popular troll. He was harassing me to scrub Twitter of evidence of my harassment.

The FBI receptionist, sounding bored (I know the feeling), says she can't help me. She tells me to call the Washington State Patrol, which seems weird. It is unmistakably a brush-off. I call the number she gives me and nobody picks up. I drop it and try to get back to work. There is no recourse.

I didn't set out to make a living writing about being abused on the Internet.

As a child, I was really more looking for an open position as, say, the burly and truculent woman-at-arms protecting an exiled queen who's disguised herself as a rag-and-bone man using cinder paste and some light sorcery. Or a flea-bitten yet perspicacious motley urchin who hides in plain sight as a harmless one-man band jackanapes in order to infiltrate the duke's winter festival and assassinate his scheming nephew with the help of my rat army. Is that hiring? Any overweening palace stewards (who are secretly a pumpkin-headed scarecrow transfigured by a witch) want to join my professional network on LinkedIn?

I was an avoider, an escaper, a fantasist. Even as an adult, all I ever wanted was to write jokes, puns, and *Game of Thrones* recaps.

Instead, here I am, sitting at my computer dealing with some fuckface's insatiable boner for harassing women. Earlier, when I said the 'violent theft of time', I meant it. Online harassment is not virtual – it is physical. Flooding in through every possible channel, it moves and changes my body: It puts me on the phone with the FBI, it gives me tension headaches and anxiety attacks; it alters my day-to-day behaviour (Am I safe? Is that guy staring at me? Is he a troll?); it alienates my friends; it steals time from my family. The goal is to traumatize me, erode my mental health, force me to quit my job.

Anytime I complain about Kevins* harassing me online, no matter how violently, sexually, or persistently, someone always pipes up with this genius theory: Rape and death threats are part and parcel of the Internet; you just can't handle it because you're oversensitive. Never mind the fact that coding sensitivity as a weakness is bizarre (what do you think this is – the Ministry of Magic under Voldemort's shadow government?), it's also simply out of step with reality. You can't do this job if you have an emotional hair trigger. Undersensitivity is practically a prerequisite.

I was at the *Stranger* for the advent of comments but prior to the ubiquity of social media, so I sat through several years of relatively innocuous variations on 'hipster douche bag' before my readers ever discovered what I look like, where I was vulnerable. In retrospect, it was bliss. I

---

* I call all anonymous Internet dill-holes 'Kevin', not because I think 'Kevin' is a bad name (you know I love you, my Kevins), but because – being from the *Home Alone* generation – it's so easy to hear a fed-up mom screaming it up a staircase. 'KEVIN, WHAT IS A "BRAZZERS" AND WHY IS IT ON MY BANK STATEMENT?'

never took those comments home with me. They were cumulatively tiresome, but they didn't sting. I think of my first real troll as the first person who crossed that line from the impersonal into the personal, the first one who made me feel unsafe, the first to worm their fingers into my meat-life and attack who I was rather than what I wrote.

At the time, I covered movies and theatre. I didn't write anything political; I didn't write about being fat or being a woman. My name is gender-ambiguous, and for the first few years of my career, many readers thought I was a man. People's assumptions tend to default to white and male, especially when the writer is loud and unapologetically critical and sharp around the edges, which was kind of my brand. (Not that women aren't naturally those things, any more or less than men are, of course, but we are aggressively socialized to be 'nice', and to apologize for having opinions.) So, while the tenor of my commenters was often snide, disdainful of the *Stranger*'s snotty teenage brand of progressivism, they stuck to hating the message, not the messenger.

Those years were liberating in a way I can barely imagine now – to be judged purely on ideas and their execution, not written off by people with preconceived notions about fat female bodies and the brains attached to them. Now I spend as much time doing damage control – playing whack-a-mole with my readership's biases against my identities (fat, female, feminist) – as I do writing new material, generating new ideas, pitching new stories, and promoting myself to new audiences. I received more bene-

fit of the doubt as an unknown regional the
I do as an internationally published polit
What could I have accomplished by now if
allowed to write? Who could I have been

I sometimes think of people's personalities as the negative space around their insecurities. Afraid of intimacy?
Cultivate aloofness. Feel invisible? Laugh loud and often.
Drink too much? Play the gregarious basket case. Hate
your body? Slash and burn others so you can climb up
the pile. We construct elaborate palaces to hide our vul-
nerabilities, often growing into caricatures of what we
fear. The goal is to move through the world without anyone knowing quite where to dig a thumb. It's a survival
instinct. When people know how to hurt you, they know
how to control you.

But when you're a fat person, you can't hide your
vulnerability, because you are it and it is you. Being fat
is like walking around with a sandwich board that says,
'HERE'S WHERE TO HURT ME!' That's why reclaiming
fatness – living visibly, declaring, 'I'm fat and I am not
ashamed' – is a social tool so revolutionary, so liberating,
it saves lives.

Unfortunately, my first troll, the first time an anonymous stranger called me 'fat' online, was years before I
discovered fat liberation. It was posted in the comments of
some innocuous blog entry on June 9, 2009, at 11:54 p.m.,
what would become a major turning point in my life:

'I'm guessing Lindy's sexual fantasies involve aliens

.at love big girls and release a hallucinogenic gas while making sweet love to a fat girl that instantly causes her to imagine herself as height/weight proportionate. With long sexy legs.'

The comment was so jarring because it was so specific. It wasn't simply dashed off in a rage – it took some thought, some creativity, some calibration. Calories were burned. The subtext that got its hooks in me the most was 'I know what you look like', implying that the author was either someone I knew who secretly despised me, or a stranger fixated enough to take the time to do research on my body. Only slightly less unsettling, the comment simultaneously sexualized me and reminded me that fat women's sexuality can only ever be a ghoulish parody. I cried. I went home early, feeling violated, and climbed into bed to binge-watch some *Law & Order*. I'd always known that my body was catnip for dicks, but up until that moment, writing had been a refuge. On paper, my butt size couldn't distract from my ideas. It hadn't even occurred to me that my legs weren't long enough. I added it to the list.

That night, I forwarded that comment to my editors and the tech team, begging for some sort of change in the comment moderation policy. How was this not a hostile work environment? How was it not gendered harassment? These people were my friends (they still are), but the best they could give me was a sympathetic brow-knit and a shrug. The Internet's a cesspool. That's just the Internet.

We all get rude comments. Can't make an Internet without getting a little Internet on your Internet!

Why, though? Why is invasive, relentless abuse – that disproportionately affects marginalized people who have already faced additional obstacles just to establish themselves in this field – something we should all have to live with just to do our jobs? Six years later, this is still a question I've yet to have answered.

At pretty much every blogging job I've ever had, I've been told (by male managers) that the reason is money. It would be a death sentence to moderate comments and block the IP addresses of chronic abusers, because it 'shuts down discourse' and guts traffic. I've heard a lot of lectures about the importance of neutrality. Neutrality is inherently positive, I'm told – if we start banning trolls and shutting down harassment, we'll all lose our jobs. But no one's ever shown me any numbers that support that claim, that harassment equals jobs. Not that I think traffic should trump employee safety anyway, but I'd love for someone to prove to me that it's more than just a cop-out.

Years later, when I moved on to a staff writer position at *Jezebel* (and trolls like sex-alien guy had become a ubiquitous potpourri), Gawker Media publisher Nick Denton unrolled a new platform called Kinja, with the express mission of 'investing in commenters'. On Kinja, any commenter could start their own blog, hosted by Gawker, which could then be mined for reposting on the main sites. Your commenter handle became the URL of your blog – so, for example, mine was lindywest.kinja. com. This was an alarming precedent from an editorial standpoint: Our employer was intentionally blurring the lines between our work as professional, experienced, vetted, paid journalists and the anonymous ramblings of the unpaid commentariat, which seemed to exist, most days, simply to antagonize us. It did not go over particularly well at the all-hands meeting. In Kinja, as the trolls quickly learned, comments are moderated by the writers, so to keep our work readable we had to dismiss and ban each one by hand. At *Jezebel*, that meant fielding a constant stream of gifs depicting graphic violence and rape. It was emotionally gruesome. But it was 'part of the job'.

The problem with handing anonymous commenters the tools of their own legitimization soon became even clearer for me. One user registered the handle 'Lindy-WestLicksMyAsshole' and began merrily commenting all over Gawker. Under Kinja, that meant there was now a permanent blog, hosted by my employer, side by side with my work, called lindywestlicksmyasshole.kinja.com. Can you imagine? At your job? That's like if your name was Dave Jorgensen and you worked at a pharmacy, and one day you got to work and right in between the fibre supplements and the seasonal candy there was a new aisle called Dave Jorgensen Is a Sex Predator. And when you complained to your manager she was like, 'Oh, you're so sensitive. It's a store! We can't change what goes in a store – we'd go out of business! We all have stuff we don't like, Dave. I don't like Salt and Vinegar Pringles, but you don't see me whining about aisle 2.'

I emailed my boss and insisted the page be taken down. She told me she'd see what she could do, but not to get my hopes up. Sure enough, Gawker higher-ups claimed it didn't violate the harassment policy. It isn't explicitly gendered or racist or homophobic. Anyway, that's just how the Internet is! If we start deleting comments because people's feelings are hurt, it'll stifle the lively comment culture that keeps the site profitable. What if LindyWestLicksMy Asshole has some really tasty anonymous tip about a congressman who did something weird with his penis? Don't you care about free speech and penis news?

It is gendered, though. Of course it's gendered. It's sexualizing me for the purpose of making me uncomfortable, of reminding my audience and colleagues and detractors that I'm a sex thing first and a human being second. That my ideas are secondary to my body. Sure, if you strip away cultural context entirely, you could construe 'Lindy WestLicksMyAsshole' as having nothing to do with gender, but that's wilful dishonesty.* I didn't have a choice, however, so I put LindyWestLicksMyAsshole out of my

---

* I did once receive an angry email from a man informing me that 'asshole' is an anti-male slur, which is about the level of understanding of female anatomy that I'd expected from someone who believes in 'reverse sexism'. (Just kidding – women poop out of our vaginas like a parrot.)

mind and tried to stay out of the comments as much as possible.

It's just the Internet. There's nothing we can do.

When I was right in that sweet spot – late *Stranger*/ early *Jezebel* – when the trolls were at full volume about my Michelin Man thorax and Dalek thighs, but my only line of defence was the foetal position, I was effectively incapacitated. I had no coping mechanisms. I felt helpless and isolated. I stayed in bed as much as possible, and kept the TV on 24/7; I couldn't fall asleep in silence. I don't know if trolls say to themselves, explicitly, 'I don't like what this lady wrote – I'm going to make sure she never leaves her apartment!' but that's what it does to the unprepared.

I know those early maelstroms pushed some of my friends away. To someone who's never experienced it, large-scale online hate is unrelatable, and complaints about it can read like narcissism. 'Ugh, what do I do with all this attention?' The times I did manage to get out and socialize, it was hard not to be a broken record, to recount tweets I'd gotten that day like a regurgitating toilet. Eventually, people got bored. Who wants to sit around in person and talk about the Internet?

Gradually, though (it took years), I got better. I learned how to weather the mob without falling out of my skin, becoming my own tedious shadow.

PLAN A: Don't click on anything. Don't read anything. Don't look at any words below any article, or any forum to which the public has any access, or any email with a vaguely suspicious subject line like 'feedback on ur work' or 'a questions about womyn' or 'feminism= female supremacy?' EVER. Because why on earth would you do that? I can understand if the Internet had just been invented Tuesday, and you sincerely thought, 'Oh, perhaps sniffmychode89 has some constructive perspective on the politics of female body hair.' However, I, Lindy West, have now been using this virtual garbage dispenser for literally twenty years, and maybe one comment in fifty contains anything other than condescending, contrarian, and/or abusive trash. I have no excuse. When I click, it is because I am a fool.

It's as if there were an international chain of delis that – no matter what franchise you went to and what you ordered and how clearly you articulated 'PAHH-STRAWWW-MEEE' – forty-nine out of fifty times they just served you a doo-doo sandwich. A big, fat, steaming scoop of doo-doo on a sesame seed bun (special sauce: doo-doo). Then you went ahead and ate the sandwich. And you didn't just eat the sandwich one time, or fifty times, or even one hundred, but you went back and ate there – with hope in your heart, paying for the privilege – every single day of your life. Thousands and thousands of days in a row. Plus, pretty much everyone you ever met had been to that deli too, and they all ate mouthfuls of straight stank doo-doo over and over again, and they told you about it. They warned you! Yet you still went back and ate the sandwich.

Because maybe this time it'd be different! Maybe – just maybe – this time you'd get the most delicious and ful-filling sandwich the world had e'er known, and the sand-wich guy would finally recognize the trenchant, incisive brilliance of your sandwich-ordering skills, and doo-doo would be abolished, and Joss Whedon would pop out of the meat freezer and hand you a trophy that said 'BEST GUY' on it and option your sandwich story for the plot of the next Avengers movie, *Captain Whatever: The Sandwich Soldier*. (Full disclosure: I do not know what an Avenger is.)

That's not what happens, though. That's never what happens. Instead, I keep slogging through forty-nine iter-ations of 'kill yourself, pig lady' per day in my Twitter mentions, because one time in 2013 the actress Holly Robinson Peete replied to my joke about Carnation instant breakfast.* Cool cost/benefit analysis, brain.

Still, I TRY not to click. I try.

PLAN B: When the temptation is too strong, when Plan A falls in the commode, I turn to the second line of defence – the mock and block. I take screen grabs of the worst ones – the ones that wish for my death, the ones that invoke my family, the ones with a telling whiff of pathos – and then repost them with a caption like 'way to go, Einstein' or 'goo goo ga ga baby man' or sometimes

---

* THIS ACTUALLY DID HAPPEN. I WOULD NOT JOKE ABOUT HOLLY ROBINSON PEETE.

just a picture of some diaper rash cream. (As Dorothy Parker or someone like that probably once said, 'Goo goo ga ga baby man is the soul of wit.') My friends and I will toss the troll around for a while like a pod of orcas with a baby seal, and once I've wrung enough validation out of it, I block the troll and let it die alone. Maybe it's cruel. I know that trolls are fundamentally sad people; I know that I've already defeated them in every substantive arena – by being smart, by being happy, by being successful, by being listened to, by being loved. Whatever. Maybe if Mr 'Kill Yourself You Fat Piece of Shit' didn't want to get mocked, shredded, and discarded, he should be more careful about how he talks to whales.

PLAN C: Wine.

Overall, my three-pronged defence holds up . . . pretty well. I am . . . okay. I cope, day to day, and honestly, there is something seductive about being the kind of person who can just take it. Challenging myself to absorb more and more hate is a masochistic form of vanity – the vestigial allure of a rugged individualism that I don't even believe in.

No one wants to need defences that strong. It always hurts, somewhere.

Besides, armour is heavy. My ability to weather online abuse is one of the great tragedies of my life.

You never get used to trolls. Of course, you are an adaptable thing – your skin thickens, your stomach settles, you learn to tune out the chatter, you cease self-Googling (mostly), but it's always just a patch. A screen. A coat of paint. It's plopping a houseplant over the dry rot. It's emotional hypothermia: Your brain can trick itself into feeling warm, but the flesh is still freezing. Medically speaking, your foot's still falling off. There's a phenomenon called 'paradoxical undressing', common when a person dies of hypothermia, wherein they become so convinced they're overheating that they peel off all their clothes and scatter them in the snow. They get colder, die faster. There's something uncanny about a cold death; a still, indifferent warping of humanity.

I struggle to conceive of the 'resilience' I've developed in my job as a good thing – this hardening inside me, this distance I've put between myself and the world, my determination to delude myself into normalcy. From the cockpit, it feels like much more of a loss than a triumph. It's like the world's most not-worth-it game show: Well, you've destroyed your capacity for unbridled happiness and human connection, but don't worry – we've replaced it with this prison of anxiety and pathological inability to relax!

Yet, it seems like the more abuse I get, the more abuse I court – baring myself more extravagantly, professing opinions that I know will draw an onslaught – because, after all, if I've already adjusted my body temperature, why not face the blizzard so that other women don't have to freeze?

Paradoxical undressing, I guess.

But it's just the Internet. There's nothing we can do.

This is my reality now. Pretty much every day, at least one stranger seeks me out to call me a fat bitch (or some pithy variation thereof). Being harassed on the Internet is such a normal, common part of my life that I'm always surprised when other people find it surprising. You're telling me you don't have hundreds of men popping into your cubicle in the accounting department of your midsized, regional dry-goods distributor to inform you that – hmm – you're too fat to rape, but perhaps they'll saw you up with an electric knife? No? Just me, then. This is the barbarism – the eager abandonment of the social contract – that so many of us face simply for doing our jobs.

I'm aware of the pull all the time: I should change careers; I should shut down my social media; maybe I can get a job in print somewhere; it's just too exhausting. I hear the same refrains from my colleagues. Not only that, but those of us who are hardest hit often wind up writing about harassment itself. I never wanted Internet trolls to be my beat – I want to write feminist polemics, jokes about wizards, and love letters to John Goodman's meaty, sexual forearms. I still want that.

I wonder if I'll ever be able to get back to work.

# Strong People Fighting Against the Elements

I never wanted to fight virtual trolls; I wanted to fight real ones. With a sword.

My fixation on the fantastical is not difficult to trace. When I was very small, my dad read out loud to me every night before bed. It was always fantasy: Tolkien, Lewis, Baum, Tolkien again. I remember him nodding off in the chair, his pace and pitch winding down like he was running out of batteries – Bifur, Bofur, Bommmmmbuuurrrrrrrrrr-rrr. To this day, if someone even mentions riding a barrel down the Celduin to Lake-town at the gates of Erebor, the Lonely Mountain (even if they're just talking about spring break), I am incapacitated by nostalgia. I made him read *The Lion, the Witch and the Wardrobe* so many times that I could recite much of it from memory – I didn't know what 'air raids' were, but I knew that when they happened, you went on a permanent vacation to a country manse where a wizard let you use his inter-dimensional closet. I wonder if we can get 'air raids' in Seattle, I thought.

Dad was a jazz pianist and an ad copywriter – an expressive baritone who was often employed as a kind of one-man, full-service jingle factory. By night, he worked in bars, sometimes seven nights a week, a lost breed of lounge entertainer who skipped dizzyingly from stand-ards to Flanders and Swann to Lord Buckley and back again. Once in a while, I still meet Seattle old-timers who blush like teenagers. 'I loved your dad. Used to go see him every night.'

My grandfather was a radio producer (*The Burns and Allen Show, Lucky Strike Hit Parade*), and in the 1940s, when he took a job at CBS, it was suggested that he change his name from the unwieldy and, perhaps, at the time, uncomfortably Austrian 'Rechenmacher' to the more radio-friendly 'West'. So my dad became Paul West Jr., and now I am Lindy West. Sometimes people think 'Lindy West' is a pseudonym. I guess they're right.

Eighty years removed, my grandparents' Old Hollywood existence seems impossibly glamorous. I imagine shim-mering laughter and natty suits. Hats on heads, hats in hat boxes. Scotch in the winter, gin in the summer. Grandma Winnie sang with Meredith Willson's orchestra, and when my dad was a little boy in the thirties, she worked in movies (under her maiden name, Winnie Parker, and her stage name, Mona Lowe), dubbing the vocal parts for Carole Lombard, Dolores del Rio, and other leading ladies who, apparently, couldn't sing. Dad had stories of going to Shirley Temple's birthday party, of nearly fainting when his dad nonchalantly introduced him to his friend Lou Costello, of Gene Autry trying to give little Paul a pony to keep in their Glendale backyard.

They drank hard – 'eating and drinking and carrying on', as my dad would say. He once emailed me a little vignette he wrote in his creative writing night class:

'The living room is the part of the house I remember least, from the inside anyway. I remember it a little better from the sidewalk in front, along Kenneth Road. I remember standing there looking at the bright gold harp that stood framed by the green brocade draperies – draperies I once hid behind when my mother and father were screaming drunk.

'I heard a dull "thunk", followed by a big crash, and when I peeked out from behind the drape, my father was lying on the living room floor, blood spurting from his big, already knobby nose. Mother and the other couple in the room, my uncle and his wife, were laughing hysterically when my grandmother came down the wide staircase. "Vas ist?" she said – with stern, Viennese dignity. "An orange," my uncle giggled, "Winnie hit him in the nose with an orange!" They were all helpless with laughter. "Be ashamed," Gramma said.'*

I never met any of those people. In fact, I've never met any family from my dad's side at all. My grandfather had a heart attack and died unexpectedly in 1953 when he was just forty-four, two days before my dad's high school graduation. There was some dispute about the burial, between the deeply Catholic Rechenmachers in southern Illinois, who wanted a Catholic funeral, and my dad's lapsed Hollywood branch, who didn't. Paul West Sr. ended up in a Catholic cemetery in Culver City, Los Angeles, where lingering animus led to nobody visiting him for the next fifty-five years, until, on a whim, my sister and I tracked down the grave. We called Dad and told him where we were. 'Golly,' he said, his voice rough.

You could tell that my dad never fully recovered from that loss (and it wasn't his last). My sister and I called him 'sad dad' – underneath the exuberance there was a towering melancholy. I sometimes told people my dad reminded me of Robin Williams, and they would assume I meant the drive to entertain, the old showbiz patter. But

---

* There's more: 'I called my blanket Hi Ho. It didn't follow me everywhere, but it was the comfort I sought when fear and injury came. On the day of the car accident on the way to the preschool, I had Hi Ho with me. It was forever stained with my blood, and while it remained beside me in my crib at night after it had been washed, the brown stains remained and tarnished the magic. The warmth was still there but the reassurance was gone. A year or so later we named our new Cocker Spaniel Hi Ho.'

that ever-present Pig-Pen cloud of kind-eyed

had four wives; my mom was the last. I think about how much faith it must have taken to keep going – to insist, over and over again, 'No! I really think it's going to work this time!' Plenty of people are irretrievably jaded after one divorce, let alone three. My dad went for it four times, and the last one stuck. You could frame that as irresponsibility or womanizing or a fear of being alone, but to me it was a distillation of his unsinkable optimism. He always saw the best in everyone – I imagine, likewise, he stood at the beginning of every romance and saw it unspooling in front of him like a grand adventure, all fun and no pain. 'Oh boy!' I can hear him saying each time. 'Isn't she just terrific?' The idea that a relationship is a 'failure' simply because it ends is a pessimist's construct anyway. Dad loved lots of people, and then found the one he loved the best.

It made sense that he was so drawn to magic and escapism, just like me. His life was beautiful and marked with loss; maybe not more than anyone else's, but when you only expect the best, heartbreak is a constant.

My mom, by contrast, never liked fantasy. When I was little, this made as much sense to me as not liking gravity, or Gordon from *Sesame Street*. 'I just like things that are true,' she'd say. 'Strong people fighting against the elements.' I grilled her so often on why she wasn't obsessed with dragons LIKE A NORMAL PERSON that it became kind of a catchphrase in our house – strong people fighting against the elements.

That made sense too. My mom's parents came from Norway: Grandma Clara first, the eldest of ten, when she was a little girl and the family homesteaded in North Dakota. We visited the old dirt farm once during a family reunion: just a hole and the remnants of the foundation and some dead grass and the big, red sun. In summer the North Dakotan prairie is flat and brown. In winter, flat and white. 'The elements', I imagine, had a seat at the table like family.

When the Depression hit and my great-grandparents just couldn't feed so many mouths, they shipped eighteen-year-old Clara back to Norway to raise two of her little sisters on her own. While Grandpa Rechenmacher's early death shaped my dad's life like a tide, absent mothers tugged on my mom's side. My great-aunt Eleanor, one of the little girls sent off to the old country, requested that 'Sometimes I Feel Like a Motherless Child' be played at her funeral, and it was.

Clara met and married my grandfather, Ole, who grew up on a farm called Gunnersveen, just down the lake. His father died in the flu pandemic of 1918, when Ole was nine. 'The boys didn't have much of a childhood,' my mom told me once, when she emailed to scold me about washing my hands during the 2009 swine flu scare (subject line:

'GERMS!'\*). In 1945, during the Nazi occupation, Grandpa Ole and his brother were among twelve resistance fighters who skied out into the dark hills to retrieve packages parachuted by an Allied spy plane – bundles of weapons, radio equipment, provisions. Strong people, elements, blah blah blah, the whole thing.

Ole and Clara married and moved to Seattle and raised seven children; my mom, Ingrid, was number six. Clara kept house – canning fruit, sewing the family's clothes, a pot of coffee perpetually perking for anyone who dropped by – and Grandpa Ole was a carpenter, never quite mastering English because, privately, he always just wanted to go home. They took in strays; sometimes as many as thirteen people lived in that three-bedroom, one-bathroom house; the kids shared beds and bathwater. 'My trick was to help my mother in the kitchen,' my mom always says when someone compliments her cooking. 'It was hard to get one-on-one time otherwise, she was so busy.' (Maybe that's why my mom stopped at one child herself.) She speaks of the cramped chaos with pride. Her ability to get by is part of her identity.

---

\* Body of email: 'My rules are: Wash your hands as soon as you get home. Then go around with a Clorox wipe and clean the doorknobs, light switches, and taps. Of course, wash before you eat and keep your hands away from your mucous membranes, including eyes. I wish I could quarantine you until this thing settles down, but I will trust you to keep yourself safe. If everybody in your house does the same, then you can feel safe at home . . . unless you accidentally let a sick person inside. Love you. Mom.'

My mother is aggressively competent. She was a nurse for forty years – yes, she will look at your infected toe – and her rigid expectations about the Correct Way to Do Things border on disordered (motto: 'If you clean your bathroom every day, you never have to clean your bathroom'). When she and my dad fell in love, he was playing the piano in bars every night, living off credit cards, occasionally accepting gin and tonics as currency, and had decorated his apartment entirely in zebra-themed bric-a-brac – due, no doubt, to some passing, impetuous whim. ('Hey, zebras are trick!') By the time I was born, a few years later, they were financially stable, he had a day job at an ad agency, and the zebra merch was limited to one vase, two paintings, a set of directors' chairs, and a life-sized stuffed zebra named Simon. You know, a reasonable amount.

He wrote a song for my mom called 'I Like You So Much Better (Than Anyone I've Ever Loved Before)' – 'Time was I took a lot of chances/on passions and romances/but you're the one who helped me get my feet back on the floor/That's why I like you so much better/than anyone I've ever loved before.'

Dad was the entertainer, but I'm funny because of my mom. She has a nurse's ease with gallows humour, sarcastic and dry; she taught me to cope with pain by chopping it up into bits small enough to laugh at. (My dad would go full Swamps of Sadness when anything went wrong. If the printer ran out of toner, he couldn't speak above a whisper for days.) When I was little, a neighbour opened a small temping agency called Multitask and, in an early stab at guerrilla marketing, purchased a vanity car registration plate that read, 'MLTITSK'. Around the house, my mom called him 'M. L. Titsky'. Later, just 'Mr Titsky'. Empirically, that's a great riff.

Once, at a neighbourhood party, she forgot that Mr Titsky wasn't actually his name, and introduced him as such to a new neighbour. Mr Titsky, it turned out, was not a comedy connoisseur.

My dad took care of unbridled enthusiasm and unconditional encouragement – everything was 'Killer!' 'WowEE!' 'You can be anything you want to be!' – while my mom's role was, 'Not today', 'Hmmm', and 'Not if you don't learn how to balance a chequebook.'* In fact, she recently told me that part of her parenting philosophy was to make sure I knew I couldn't be anything.

'Well, you can't,' she said. 'I didn't want you to be disappointed.'

If my dad supported us with words, head in the clouds, my mom supported us with structure, roots in the ground. That degree of harmonious opposition has to fulfil some cosmic archetype. (Not that my mom would allow such arcane silliness to be discussed in her house.)

Between those far-flung poles – escapism vs. realism,

---

* Still haven't. Only 20 per cent clear on the definition, to be honest.

glamour vs. austerity, wild hope vs. Nordic practicality – I grew.

People say to me all the time, 'I couldn't do what you do; I couldn't cope with trolls,' but it's just part of my job. I bet they could if they had to.

Once in a while, though, I wonder: Is it more than that? Did I somehow stumble into a job – one that didn't even exist when I was born in 1982 – for which I am supremely, preternaturally suited? I do fight monsters, just like I always dreamed, even if they are creeps in basements who hate women instead of necromancers in skull-towers who hate lady knights. Without my mom, would I have the grit to keep going? Without my dad, would I have the idealism to bother?

# The Day I Didn't Fit

One time, I flew first class on an aeroplane, because when I checked in they offered me a fifty-dollar upgrade, and when you are a fat person with fifty dollars and somebody offers you a 21-inch recliner instead of a 17-inch trash compacter, you say YES. It was a new world up there, in front of that little magic curtain, among the lordlings. I was seated next to a businessman in leather shoes that cost more than my car, and behind a man who kept angrily attempting to sell a boat over the phone even after they told us to stop making phone calls.

The first rule of first class, apparently, is that there are no rules. (The second rule is don't let the poor people use the rich people bathroom.)

I wondered if my fellow first-classers – all virility and spreadsheets – could discern that I was a fraud, that I could only afford the upgrade because my job covered the rest of my ticket. I may have betrayed myself when the flight attendant asked if I'd like a 'special drink' before takeoff and I yelled, 'A SPECIAL DRINK?' and then ordered three. Why just have coffee like some row-26 peasant when you could have coffee, ginger ale, and a mimosa?! This, as I'd been assured by the airline industry, was the life.

As the flight progressed, first class got less exciting. At some point, once the initial thrill of being adjacent to a four-figure boat sale had worn off, I realized: These special drinks weren't remotely special. This roast beef sandwich, though presented with a *cloth napkin*, was in no way luxurious. (Also, 'sandwich' is a rather generous term for a microwaved wad of airborne grey beef.) My first-class chair wasn't a plush throne stuffed with Richard Branson's hair, as air travel's mythology would have you believe – it was simply an average-sized chair with a human amount of leg room (as opposed to economy seats, which are novelty-sized file drawers with a elfin amount of leg room). It wasn't unbearable. The highest praise I can give it is that it was adequate. It had succeeded at being a chair instead of a flying social experiment about the limits of human endurance. The rich aren't paying for luxury – they're paying for basic humanity.

For me, the primary advantage of flying first class was that it precluded the dread. I didn't know about the dread until the fall of 2013 – the first time I got on a plane and discovered that I didn't quite fit in the seat. I've always been fat, but I was the fat person that still mostly fit. While

I couldn't fit into regular-lady clothes (more bejewelled tunics covered with skulls, cherries, and antique postage stamps, please!), and I had to be careful with butt safety (I once Godzilla'd an entire lunch setting while trying to sidle through a Parisian café), I was still the kind of fat person who could move through the straight-sized world without causing too many ripples. Until I couldn't.

It had been an incredibly busy year for me professionally – I'd probably flown twenty times in the preceding eight months, and there's nothing like a steady diet of stress and airport food to keep the waistline trim – and one day I sat down and it just didn't work. I was on a flight home from Texas, and the flight out there had been fine. Suddenly, on the return flight, I had to cram myself in. I mean, I know I ate that brisket, but I was only gone for two days! I'm no butt scientist (just two credits away, though!), but how fast could a person's butt possibly grow?

If you've never tried cramming your hips into an angular metal box that's an inch or two narrower than your flesh (under the watchful eye of resentful tourists), then sitting motionless in there for five hours while you fold your arms and shoulders up like a dying orchid in order to be as unobtrusive as possible, run, don't walk. It's like squeezing your bones in a vice. The pain makes your teeth ache. I once spent a tearful eight-hour flight from Oslo to Seattle convinced I could feel my femurs splintering like candy canes. It hurts.

Much worse than any physical pain is the anxiety – the

dread – of walking up the aisle and not knowing what type of plane you're on. Every model has different seat widths and belt lengths, which also vary from airline to airline. Am I going to fit this time? Will I have to ask for a seat-belt extender? Is this a 17-incher or an 18-incher? Is the person next to me going to hate me? Does everyone on this plane hate me? I paid money for this?

I have, in my life, been a considerably thinner person and had a fat person sit next to me on a plane. I have also, more recently, been the fat person that makes other travellers' faces fall. Being the fat person is worse.

Here's how I board a plane. I do not book a ticket unless I can be assured a window seat – I will happily sit in the very back row, or change my flight to the buttcrack of dawn – because the window well affords me an extra couple of inches in which to compress my body to give my neighbour as much space as possible. It's awkward and embarrassing to haul and cram myself in and out of the seat, so I also prefer the window because I'm not blocking anyone's bathroom access. I've learned from experience that emergency exit rows and bulkhead rows are often narrower, so those are out. My preflight anxiety begins the day before, when I remember that I have a trip coming up. I arrive at least two hours early, even for domestic flights, to preclude any risk of having to run, because the only thing worse than being fat on a plane is being fat, red, sweaty, and huffing on a plane. I go to the bathroom multiple times before boarding because, again, I avoid getting out of my seat at all costs, even on international flights. (The path from fat-shaming to deep vein thrombosis is short and slick.) I linger by the gate so I can board as early as possible and be the first one in my row; that way I don't have to make anyone wait in the aisle while I get my body folded up and squared away. As I pass the flight attendants at the front of the plane I ask, discreetly, if I can have a seat-belt extender, to minimize the embarrassment of having to ring the call button once I'm seated and let my seatmates know they're next to the too-big kind of fat person. Finally, I press myself up against the wall like a limpet and try to go to sleep, avoiding any position in which I might snore and remind everyone about my fat, lumpy windpipe.

That's the amount of forethought, anxiety, and emotional energy that goes into every single flight. Fat people are not having fun on planes. There is no need to make it worse.

Just a month or two after the first time I didn't fit, on a crack-of-dawn flight from New York City to Seattle, I had my first ever, um, disagreement with a seatmate. Despite my online irascibility, I'm pathologically polite in person, so face-to-face hostility is foreign to me. I'd almost missed the plane – I was that person staggering on board just before the doors closed – and I'm sure this dude thought he was going to have the three-seat row all to himself. He was about my age, maybe midthirties, an average kind of guy. Probably works in an office; hangs out at, like, an

Irish pub because he's too old for clubs but still wants to hit on chicks; has always wanted to learn to surf but will never get around to it. I don't know, just a guy. I flashed him an apologetic smile and pointed to the middle seat. 'Hey, sorry, I'm over there.' He didn't respond or make eye contact, just glared blankly at my hips. Then, as I went to put my bag in the overhead locker, I heard him mutter something sour.

'[Something something], say excuse me.'

I froze. Was someone being a dick to me? In person? At seven a.m.? In an enclosed space? For no reason? When I have a hangover? And we're about to be stuck next to each other for the next five hours? I'm used to men treating me like garbage virtually, or from fast-moving cars, but this close-quarters face-to-face shit-talking was a jarring novelty.

'What?' I asked.

'Nothing,' he muttered, still refusing to look at me.

'No,' I said. If I'm going to make a living telling women to stick up for themselves, I need to do it too. 'You said something. What did you say?'

'Nothing,' he repeated.

'No,' I repeated. 'What did you say? Tell me.'

'I said,' he snapped, 'that if you want someone to move, it helps to say "excuse me" and then get out of the way. You told me to move and then you just –' He gestured with a large circular motion at my body.

'I'm putting my bag in the overhead locker,' I said,

anxiety thundering in my ears. 'You know, because that's how planes work?'

'Yeah,' he said, dripping with disdain. 'Okay.'

He stood up so I could slide into the middle seat, keeping his gaze fixed on the far bank of windows, avoiding my eye contact. I sat, trying not to touch him. My head felt like a hot-air balloon. I hadn't said 'excuse me' yet because I was still in the process of putting my bag in the overhead locker. The 'excuse me' part of the transaction comes when you ask the other person to get up. I hadn't leaned over him or touched him or dropped anything on him. No éclairs had tumbled out of my cleavage and into his hair. Was a preemptive 'sorry' really not enough? Had I violated some custom I was unaware of? Had I fallen through a tesseract and into a dimension where 'sorry' means 'No offence, but you have a fuck-you personality'? If not, I could not fathom where I'd gone wrong.

The last few passengers boarded and they closed the doors. No one came to claim our window seat, so I slid over, saying, 'Looks like there's no one in the middle seat, so you won't actually have to sit next to me. Since I apparently bother you so much.'

'Sounds great to me,' he droned, eyes front.

As soon as he fell asleep (with his mouth open like a nerd), I passive-aggressively jarred his foot with my backpack and then said, 'Oh, excuse me,' because I am an adult (and he loves to hear 'excuse me'!). We ignored each other for the rest of the flight.

It felt alien to be confronted so vocally and so publicly (and for such an arbitrary reason), but it also felt familiar. People say the same kind of thing to me with their eyes on nearly every flight – this guy just chose to say it with his mouth.

This is the subtext of my life: 'You're bigger than I'd like you to be.' 'I dread being near you.' 'Your body itself is a breach of etiquette.' 'You are clearly a fucking fool who thinks that cheesecake is a vegetable.' 'I know that you will fart on me.'

Nobody wants to sit next to a fat person on a plane. Don't think we don't know.

That's why – to return to my first-class flight – my foray into 'luxury' was so disheartening. It wasn't a taste of the high life so much as an infuriating illumination of how dismal it is to fly any other way. I realized: Oh. Flying first class wasn't intrinsically special, but it was the first time in recent memory that I've felt like a human being on a plane.

We put up with economy class because most of us have no choice – we need to get from here to there and we want cheaper and cheaper tickets. I can't blame airlines for trying to stay in business by compressing as many travellers as possible into economy like a Pringles can lined with meat glue. It seems like a straightforward business decision, which is why it's confusing, as a fat person, to hear so much about how I, personally, have ruined air travel. There are entire blogs devoted to hating fat people on planes – describing their supposed transgressions and physical particulars in grotesque, gleeful detail, posting clandestine photos, and crowing about the verbal abuse that posters claim to have heaped on their bigger neighbours. As though there were a time when 1) there were no fat people, and 2) everyone passionately loved flying.

As a counterpoint, I would like to lodge a gentle reminder that air travel has been terrible for a long time. It's terrible because a plane is just a flying bus, trapped in an eternal rush hour, with recycled farts and vaporized child sputum instead of air, seats barely wider than the average human pelvis, and a bonus built-in class hierarchy. Barring a brief period in the fifties and sixties, when aeroplanes were reportedly flying, smoke-choked bacchanals staffed by Bond girls wearing baby onesies, air travel has been a study in discomfort giving way to ever more profitable methods of making people uncomfortable. That has nothing to do with fat people's bodies.

I'm sure some fat people are fat by their own hand, without any underlying medical conditions, but a lot of other fat people are fat because they're sick or disabled. Unless you're checking every human being's blood test results before they pull up Kayak.com, you do not know which fat people are which. Which means, inevitably, if you think fat people are 'the problem' (and not, say, airlines hoping to squeeze out extra revenue, or consumers who want cheap airline tickets without sacrificing amenities), you are penalizing a significant number of human beings emotionally and financially for a disease or disability that already complicates their lives. Ethically, that's fucked up.

That dude next to me didn't call me fat to my face. I don't even know if that's what was bothering him, although I recognized the way he looked at my body (my body, not my face, not once, not ever). I can't be sure why that guy was mad at me, but I know why people are usually mad at me on planes. I know that he disliked me instantly, he invented a reason to be a jerk to me, and then he executed it. More importantly, I see other people staring those same daggers at other fat people's bodies every day, in the sky and on the ground, and congratulating themselves for it, as though they're doing a righteous public service.

Even less popular than being fat on a plane, I soon discovered, was talking about being fat on a plane with anything but grovelling, poo-eating penitence.

Not long after it happened, I wrote about 'say excuse me' guy in a little essay for *Jezebel*, about holiday air travel, not expecting anything beyond the usual 'eat less/exercise more' anti-fat backlash. It was a vulnerable story, and a sympathetic one, I thought, about the low-grade hostility that fat people face every day (and about the debilitating self-doubt bred by micro-aggressions – does this person really hate me or am I being oversensitive?), and I told it plainly, as it happened. I assumed that people could connect with me, the person, and potentially break down some of the prejudice that makes fat people such popular pariahs. The actual response caught me off guard, though it shouldn't have.

Without considering for a moment that I might have interpreted my own experiences accurately – that this very simple and famously common interaction, an aeroplane passenger feeling resentful about sitting next to a fat person, might be true – readers bent over backwards to construct elaborate alternate narratives in which I was the villain. I was the one being rude, by saying 'sorry' instead of 'excuse me'. (What rule is that?) I had smothered him with my gut when I reached up to stow my bag. (Ew, as if I like touching people.) I had delayed the flight with my entitled, irresponsible failure to show up on time. (I was there within the boarding window, I just wasn't early, the way I like to be.) I was the last person on the plane (nope). I was still drunk, looking for a fight, ranting and raving and reeking of booze. (What do I look like – a freshman?)

In the same breath that commenters were telling me I was overreacting, I was delusional, I was lying – a man couldn't possibly have been hostile to me on an aeroplane – they were also chiming in with and commiserating over their own anecdotes about the horrors of flying near disgusting, smelly, presumptuous fat people. So which is it? Are fat people treated just fine on planes or is flying with fat people such a torment that it warrants a public crusade?

Part of writing is choosing which details to include and which to discard. Part of reading is deciding whether or not you can trust your narrator. The Internet made it very clear, very quickly, once my post went up, that trusting me was not on the table. I didn't bother to mention, for instance, that the dude was sitting with his legs splayed wide in classic 'MAN'S STEAMING BALLS COMING THROUGH' fashion, with his foot in the middle foot-well (my footwell) where I'd stowed my backpack. (If I had, I would have been accused of feminist hysteria, the way women who call out subway 'manspreading' have been.) I didn't waste words on the fact that when they closed the cabin doors and it became clear that our window seat was going to be unoccupied, I moved my back-pack to the window seat, where I'd already been sitting. So, yeah, I jostled the guy's foot when I moved my bag, because the guy's foot was blocking my bag. The guy didn't even wake up. I thought it was tedious and unneces-sary exposition (and, if you're still awake at this point in this boring-ass paragraph, you'll see that I was right). I assumed that *Jezebel* readers would trust that I am as I have always presented myself – a kind, pragmatic, non-violent, reasonable human being – and read my story with a modicum of empathy, or at least the benefit of the doubt.

Within hours of my post cycling through the Internet sausage factory, I was barraged with bizarre fictions on Twit-ter: I had stumbled on to the plane drunk, delayed takeoff as I screamed at the guy to move, sat on him, viciously kicked him with my wide-calf boot, brutally beaten him with my backpack, continued to harass and mock him for the dura-tion of the flight as he quivered in terror and pretended to sleep, then eagerly libelled him on the Internet. One particularly putrid community of misogynists threatened to 'report me to the FBI' for 'assault and battery in a federal airspace'. (LOL, go for it, sluggers.) They also coordinated a (temporarily successful) effort to Google bomb my name so that their 'article' – 'Fat Feminist Lindy West Goes Berserk Because She No Longer Fits in Airplane Seats' – came up on the first page of search results.

Here's an excerpt from that totally reasonable and not-at-all-bigoted-because-fatphobia-isn't-a-real-thing reaction to my article ([sic] throughout):

> Is this who we want having influence in our country? Society must realize there are consequences to fat feminist beliefs. They range from the concrete (not fitting on aeroplanes) to creating a class of perennial female victims-seekers who have no notion of personality responsibility. Instead of focusing on self-improvement, they seek to blame everyone else for their problems, even innocent men on aeroplanes who have their property damaged from the canckled legs of deranged women.

On a different site, a commenter wrote: 'Man FUCK HER. I wouldn't want to stoop to feminist levels and wish bodily harm – castration/acid burning her face, etc. – on her, but if I did, then I'd say I wish that Buffalo Bill taught her a lesson or two.'

And another: 'My God, what a putrid and deluded

fucking cunt. I'm so glad that her health decisions that are none of my business will see her in an early grave. I'm sure when she loses her legs from diabetes or has a heart attack at forty due to lard clogged arteries that will be the patriarchy's fault too. Bitch.'

Very astute, boys. I was probably just imagining the whole thing. I'm certainly not an adult human being who's been successfully reading social cues for thirty years. And we certainly don't have any evidence of general animosity toward fat people, particularly fat people on planes.

Before the day I didn't fit, this conversation was largely an abstraction for me. My stance was the same as it is now (if people pay for a service, it's the seller's obligation to accommodate those people and provide the service they paid for), but I didn't understand what that panicky, uncertain walk down the aisle actually felt like. How inhumane it is.

I'm telling you this not to garner sympathy or pity, or even to change your opinion about how aeroplanes should accommodate larger passengers. I'm just telling you, human to human, that life is complicated and fat people are trying to live. Same as you. Reasons I have had to fly within the past five years: For work (often). To see beloved friends get married. To speak to college students about rape culture and body image. To hold my father's hand while he died. I'm sorry, but I'm not constraining and rearranging my life just because no one cares enough to make flying accessible to all bodies.

Airlines have no incentive to fix this problem until

we, collectively, as a society, demand it. We don't insist on a solution because it's still culturally acceptable to be cruel to fat people. When even pointing out the problem – saying, 'my body does not fit in these seats that I pay for' – returns nothing but abuse and scorn, how can we ever expect that problem to be addressed? The real issue here isn't money, it's bigotry. We don't care about fat people because it is okay not to care about them, and we don't take care of them because we think they don't deserve care.

It's the same lack of care that sees fat people dying from substandard medical attention, being hired at lower rates and convicted at higher ones, and being accused of child abuse for feeding their children as best they can.

You can't fix a problem by targeting its victims. Even if you hate fat people with all your heart, if you actually want to get us out of 'your' armrest space, defending our humanity is the only pragmatic solution. Because no matter how magnificently you resent them, you cannot turn a fat person into a thin person in time for the final boarding call (nor a full bladder into an empty one, nor a crying baby into a baked potato). The only answer is to decide we're worth helping.

# Chuckletown, USA, Population: Jokes

For English requirement in high school, I took a class called 'Autobiography', because it was taught by my favourite teacher. I didn't have anything remotely noteworthy to say about myself (*Today after Basketball I Tried Red Powerade Instead of Blue Powerade but I Think I'll Switch Back Tomorrow, I Don't Know, I Am Also Considering Mandarin Blast: A Life*, by Lindy West), nor was I particularly interested, at the time, in reading the memoirs of others (*I Read This Entire Book about Florence Griffith Joyner and It Did Not Contain a Single Gryphon, Chimera, or Riddling Sphinx, BOOOOOOOO: A Life*, by Lindy West). My friends and I signed up for all of Ms Harper's classes religiously, though, so 'Autobiography' it was.

Ms Harper was one of those young, cool teachers who

understood jokes and wore normal clothes, and you could tell she still had a social life and probably went to bar trivia and maybe even a Tori Amos concert once in a while for a fun gals' night. We were mildly infatuated with her because she was a relatable human being in the alienating, chaotic landscape of public high school – unlike, say, the primordial Spanish teacher who seemed to be carved out of desk, whose favourite lesson plan was to turn on *Lambada: The Forbidden Dance**\* and doze off. Ms Harper was the kind of baby-showers-and-brunch friend I imagined myself having mimosas with when I was, like, thirty-two. (Coincidentally, I ran into Ms Harper at a movie theatre when I was thirty-two, moved to giddily embrace her, and she did not remember me. FINE. IT'S FINE.)

For the final exam, we were supposed to make a presentation, ten or fifteen minutes long, about anything we wanted. Any hobby or interest that we felt made us unique – whatever our thing was. One guy showed us his scuba gear and talked about why he liked scuba diving. (I don't remember, but 'fish,' probably?) A quiet, unassuming dude brought in a massive easel, on which he displayed his painstakingly detailed step-by-step guide to 'Gettin' Dipped', which was a kind of proto-Tom Haverford swagger manual ('Step One: Get Money'). The band kids

---

\* Once we got bored of *Lambada*, a few months into the school year, he'd switch to a Spanish dub of the 1996 Michael Keaton human cloning comedy *Multiplicity*, or *Mis Otros Yo*.

showed off their spit valves, and the outdoor-education kids bragged about their search and rescue pagers and someone served Salvadoran pupusas that she made with her mom.

As the date of my presentation loomed, so did my despair. Anything that could remotely be considered 'my thing' was either too childish, too insignificant, or too dorky to say out loud in front of a room full of teenagers. What – collecting miniature ceramic cat families? Choir? Feminist young adult high fantasy? I might as well do my presentation on 'my binky' or 'calling the cops on Jeremy's house party' or '[whatever style of jeans is most unfashionable during your era, deep in the future, in which scholars and kings are no doubt still reading this classic book]'.

How are you supposed to choose what represents you as a human being when you have no idea who you are yet? When I asked myself the question honestly – what is my thing? – the only answer I could come up with was that I liked watching TV, eating hot sandwiches, and hanging out with my friends. Tragically, I was not enough of a visionary at the time to turn 'Leah, Hester, Emily, Aditi, Tyler, Claire and a panini' into an oral report, so I was like, shrug, guess I'll go with 'watching TV'.

I really did. I stayed up all night the night before my presentation, two VCRs whirring hot on the floor of our basement, editing together a montage of all of my top clips. I arranged them chronologically – not by release date, but in the order in which I'd loved them – from my favourite when I was a toddler (John Cleese guesting on *The Muppet*

*Show*) all the way up to what my friends and I were having giggle fits over at the time a sketch series called (*Mr Show*). Even though this was pre-YouTube, pre-torrenting, pre-home-editing-software, I had everything I needed on hand: Since sixth grade, I'd been obsessively recording off the TV, and had amassed a mountain of painstakingly labelled VHS tapes. I taped David Letterman and Conan every night. I taped *Talk Soup*, *SNL*, *Politically Incorrect*, O'Brien every stand-up special on the Comedy Central channel, *Fawlty Towers*, *Garfield's Halloween Adventure*, the earliest episodes of *The Daily Show*. Anything I thought was funny, I taped it, and watched it over and over, hoping to absorb its powers.

I don't remember everything that ended up in my montage, but I know I used the part in *Bill & Ted's Excellent Adventure* (favourite movie, 1989 to present), when Bill's trying to keep his stepmom from noticing that he and Keanu Reeves are forcing six kidnapped historical figures to do his chores: 'These are my friends...Herman the Kid, Socrates Johnson, Bob Genghis Khan...' There was this Conan clip I thought was so fucking funny – a character called the 'Narcoleptic Craftsman', where the entire bit was that the Narcoleptic Craftsman would fall asleep during a woodworking segment and cut all his fingers off. 'See,' Conan's sidekick Andy Richter deadpanned, 'have a craftsman on, OR have a narcoleptic on. It's when you combine the two that you get something like this.'

I cut all my treasures together on one tape, wrote up

some hasty trash about how my 'favourite pastime is laughing,'* claimed that this was a highly academic audit of 'the evolution of my sense of humor', and sped to class. As I floundered through my speech and the tape rolled, I could see disappointment solidifying on Ms Harper's face. She liked me – she said I was smart, and a good writer – and this was such an obvious cop-out. My tape was too long, and the bell rang before it was over. People wandered out without finishing it, bored. For years afterwards, thinking of that presentation made me a little sick.

The following year, just months before graduation, I met a girl named Meagan in Shakespeare class. We ran in overlapping circles, but somehow had never connected. From afar, I found her intimidating, and she never noticed me at all. I had that effect on people. In close quarters, though, assigned to the same group project, we were platonically, electrically smitten – both of us, I think, relieved to finally meet someone else who was 'a bit much' for people in all the same ways. Too loud, too awkward, too boisterous, too intense. Meagan is aggressively exuberant. She doesn't say anything that isn't funny, which sounds like an exaggeration, but isn't. She was bold in ways that I had never imagined, even though I'd shrugged off most of my shyness years before: Meagan was honest. She wasn't nice to people she didn't like. She talked back to authority

---

* [Fire hose of vomit]

figures if she thought they were feeding her bullshit. She delivered hard 'no's and didn't waver.

I discovered that Meagan was an obsessive comedy archivist, just like me. It was uncanny: Her bedroom was stacked with fat loaves of VHS tapes, also painstakingly labelled (in her handwriting weirdly like mine), that she'd been recording off the TV for years, just like me. We'd drive around for hours in my Volvo, listening to Mitch Hedberg and David Cross; with the advent of Napster, we could make each other entire mix-CDs that were just audio clips from *The Simpsons*. Meagan spent fifty dollars on eBay – an exorbitant amount of money at the time – to get a bootleg VHS copy of every *Tenacious D* episode. We wore the tape out. Within months, our vocal cadence merged, until even we couldn't tell our voices apart, and sometimes we went so long without saying anything that wasn't a reference or an inside joke that we might as well have been speaking some feral bog twin language. We won 'funniest' in the senior class poll.

We were fucking unbearable.

Comedy has always been a safe harbour for the 'a bit much'es of the world. The things that made Meagan and me horrible to be around – the caterwauling, the irreverence, the sometimes inappropriate honesty, the incessant riffing – aren't just welcome in comedy, they're fundamental. For me, as a kid who felt lonely, ugly, simultaneously invisible and too visible, comedy felt like a friend. That's its greatest magic – more than any other art form, it forces you to interact with it; it forces you to feel not alone. Because you can't be alone when someone's making you laugh, physically reaching into your body and eliciting a response. Comedy is also smart. It speaks the truth. It was everything I wanted to be. Plus, if you're funny, it doesn't matter what you look like.

During college, in Los Angeles, I went to comedy shows as often as I could (usually alone; my roommates didn't much care): Patton Oswalt working out new material at M Bar, Paul F. Tompkins singing 'Danny Boy' at Largo, Mitch Hedberg at the Improv soon before he died. It was rapturous. We were between comedy booms at the time, and I didn't understand that normal people weren't starstruck by Marc Maron and Greg Proops and Maria Bamford. Why were they so accessible? Don't they keep the celebrities in a bunker somewhere? Why was Bob Odenkirk, the most important man in the world, sitting next to me at the bar, where anyone could talk to him? How was it possible that I just accidentally body-slammed Bobcat Goldthwait outside the bathroom? Also, was he okay? (He is very small!)

Once, at the Paul F. Tompkins Show (which I never missed), I was seated at a cocktail table next to Andy Richter and his wife, Sarah Thyre. 'Have a craftsman on,' I thought, 'OR have a narcoleptic on. Have a craftsman on, OR have a narcoleptic on!' I ran to the bathroom and called Meagan. 'Fuck you,' she said.

I wanted to be immersed in comedy – the creation

of it and the consumption of it – all the time. I couldn't sleep without Ricky Gervais and Stephen Merchant's XFM radio show playing; I've probably fallen asleep to Gervais's voice more than my own mother's. I never wanted to do stand-up, particularly, though I certainly nursed an idealized notion of how 'fun' it would be to hang out in comedy club greenrooms ('HAHAHAHAHAH' – Me now). My real Xanadu was the TV writers' room. I couldn't believe that people got paid to sit around a table and riff with their friends – building from scratch the kind of rich, brilliant TV universes that had felt like family to me growing up.

I graduated in 2004 with an English degree and a case of impostor syndrome so intense that I convinced myself I 'didn't have enough ideas' to become a writer of any kind.

Instead, when people asked me what I wanted to do with my life, I'd say this: 'Well, I only have one skill, which is that I know how to make sentences, kind of, but I don't know, I'm not, like, a writer.' A COMPELLING PITCH, YOUNG WEST. With no other options, or ideas, or interests, I took an unpaid internship at a free 'parenting magazine' in the Valley. It was essentially a packet of coupons and ads for backyard clowns, padded with a handful of 'articles' written by interns (me) and a calendar highlighting what time Three Dog Night would be appearing at the Antelope Valley Fair (four p.m.). There were three people in editorial (including me), and what seemed like hundreds in sales.

Despite still being a child myself in, like, nine out of ten ways (exception: boobs), I threw myself gamely into the 'job'. If I'm going to sit in a windowless suburban office for twenty hours a week for zero dollars, I might as well try to get some clips out of it. The slimy Young Businessman who owned the place didn't care that I was alarmingly, dangerously unqualified to dispense parenting advice, so I was assigned pieces on anything from 'what to do if your child is a bully' to 'should you bank your baby's umbilical cord blood?' (I believe my answers were, 'IDK, talk to it?' and 'uuuuuuhhhhhhhhhhhhhhhhhhhhhhhhhhhhhhhhhhhhh hhhhhhhhhhhhhhhhhhhhhhhhhhhhhhhhhhhhhhhhhhhhh hhhhhhhhhhhhhhhhhhhhhhhhhhhhhhhhhhhhhhhhhhhhh hhhhhhhhhhhhhhhhhhhhhhhhhhhhhhhhhhhhhhhhhhhhh hhhhhhhhhhhhhhhhhhhhhhhhhhhhhhhhhhhhhhhhhhhhh hhhhhhhhhhhhhhhhhhhhh............. yes?' respectively.) I can only hope that no families were destroyed during my tenure. To be fair, though, DON'T GET YOUR BABY BLOOD TIPS FROM A CLOWN PAMPHLET.

I finally quit the day one of the slimers made me drive to a lumberyard in South Pasadena to pick up a cord of firewood for his motivational corporate firewalking side business. This was *not* in the terms of my internship. He instructed me to drop the wood off – and unload it myself, alone, log by log – at this creepy, barren porn-condo that apparently was Slimer Firewalking Inc.'s HQ. He touched my arm, slipped me twenty dollars, and asked, huskily, if I'd ever walked on hot coals. 'Yeah, no,' I said, moving toward the door.

'Do you want to?' he called after me. 'It'll change you.'

'I'm good!'

In retrospect, I should have sued that place for all of its dirty, on-fire clown money. Instead, I gave up on L.A. and moved back home.

Seattle, in 2005, had our own little comedy boom. I started hanging around open-mic nights because Hari Kondabolu – college roommate of a friend – had moved to town and joined our social circle. (Coincidentally, he lived in a house with the guy who brought the scuba gear into Autobiography class, because Seattle is only four people big.) When I looked at Hari's Friendster profile, before we'd even met, and discovered that he was a comic, I thought, 'Holy shit. I'm about to have a comedy friend.'

People who were around at the time still talk about that scene with reverence. It did feel special – some lucky confluence of the right people, the right rooms, the right mentorship, the right crowds, the right branding. Comics did weird, experimental stuff and filled seats at each other's shows. You could feel something happening. Meanwhile, the national comedy boom was percolating – Louis CK was becoming a household name, people were starting to realize the potential of podcasting.

At those early Seattle shows, a few faces were ubiquitous: Hari, Emmett Montgomery, Dan Carroll, Derek Sheen, Andy Peters, Scott Moran, Andy Haynes (WHO

WAS ALSO IN AUTOBIOGRAPHY CLASS OH MY GOD), and Ahamefule J. Oluo, a tall, gloomy single dad who quickly formed a writing partnership with Hari and was folded into our social circle as well.

I did stand-up once in a while too, usually at Hari's urging, but knew pretty quickly that it wasn't my thing. I hated telling the same jokes over and over, and I hated the grind, which means I never tried hard enough to actually get good. (If you've never done stand-up in a brightly lit pizzeria at six p.m. in front of four people who were not informed that there would be comedy, try it, it's great.) I liked performing, though, and eventually I started hosting the Seattle outpost of The Moth, a live storytelling show – three hours of crowd work twice a month. I was good at it.

Through some dark sorcery, I managed to parlay my parenting magazine clips into an internship in the theatre department of the *Stranger*, which turned into freelance writing work, which turned into a staff position as a film critic, where I wrote goofy movie reviews and a column covering Seattle comedy called 'Chuckletown, USA, Population: Jokes.' A representative excerpt:

*WEDNESDAY 6/1*
*ROB DELANEY*
*Rob Delaney is the best person on Twitter. He loves pussy. Rendezvous, 10 pm, $15, 21+.*

I was going to comedy shows at night, interviewing comics, watching movies and TV for a living, and writing jokes in the newspaper all day. Then, one day, it struck me: I did it. I got paid to watch comedy and make people laugh. In just seven years, I'd actually lived up to that stupid Autobiography presentation.

Like, Toby isn't a professional scuba diver and Jessica C. isn't an itinerant bassoonist and Jessica R. doesn't run a Salvadoran pupusa stand, although maybe she should get on that already because those things were hella good. I did hear a rumour that 'Gettin' Dipped' guy is a male model now, so technically he is professionally 'dipped' (touché), but other than that, I couldn't think of anyone else from class whose presentation actually foreshadowed the course of their life. Not that they were supposed to, of course – it was just a throwaway assignment. But for me, who'd struggled to define myself for so many years, it was an unexpected wonder to realize that my presentation wasn't an embarrassment – it was a goddamn prophecy.

At the Bridgetown Comedy Festival in Portland (in 2010, its third year), I found myself standing next to Ahamefule in the back of a club, watching an old friend's set. The guy was doing a bit about sex, or maybe online dating – I don't remember the premise, but I remember that the punch line was 'herpes', and it was killing. It wasn't a self-deprecating joke about the comic's own herpes. It was about other people. People with herpes are gross, ha ha ha. Girls with herpes are sluts. I hope I never accidentally have sex with a gross slut with herpes! Let's all laugh at people with herpes and pretend like none of the people in the room has herpes, even though, depending on which statistics you believe, anywhere from 15 per cent to 75 per cent of the people in the room have herpes. Let's force all of those people to laugh along too, ha ha ha.

It's a lazy joke, but a common one, and a year earlier I might not have thought anything of it. Just then, though, a friend was going through some shit – a partner had lied about his STI status, then slipped the condom off without her consent, and a few weeks later she erupted in sores so painful she couldn't walk or sit, move or not move. She was devastated, not just because of the violation, the deception, and the pain, but because the disease is so stigmatized. She was sure she'd never be able to date again. It seemed entirely possible to her that she might be alone forever, and, she thought, maybe she deserved it. 'You know,' I remember telling her, 'it's just a skin condition. A rash, like acne or hives or eczema. Are those shameful?' I rubbed her back while she sobbed in my car.

That interaction was fresh in my mind as I watched this dude – who is a funny, good person – tell his joke, and I thought about all the people in the audience who were plastering smiles over their feelings of shame, of being tainted and ruined forever, in that moment. I thought about my friend, who – unless you believe recreational sex is an abomination and STIs are God's dunce caps – didn't 'deserve' this virus. Neither did anyone else in that room. So, did she deserve to have her trauma be the butt of a joke? Even if you could milk a cheap laugh out of the word 'herpes', was it worth it to shore up the stigma that made real people's lives smaller and harder? Was the joke even that funny anyway?

Stigma works like this: Comic makes people with herpes the butt of his joke. Audience laughs. People with herpes see their worst fears affirmed – they are disgusting, broken, unlovable. People without herpes see their worst instincts validated – they are clean, virtuous, better. Everyone agrees that no one wants to fuck someone with herpes. If people with herpes want to object, they have to 1) publicize the fact that they have herpes, and 2) be accused of oversensitivity, of ruining the fun. Instead, they stay quiet and laugh along. The joke does well. So well that maybe the comedian writes another one.

I cycled through that system over and over in my head. It was maddeningly efficient – what were people supposed to do? More broadly, in a nation where puritanical gasbags have a death grip on our public education system, can we really expect ironclad safe sex practices in people from whom comprehensive sex ed has been withheld? Blaming and shaming people for their own illnesses has always been the realm of moralists and hypocrites, of the anti-sex status quo. Isn't comedy supposed to be the vanguard of counterculture? Of speaking truth to power? The longer

I turned it over the more furious I became. Why do we all just laugh along with this?

I moved close to Aham's ear and said, over the boisterous crowd, 'You know, I could have herpes.'

He looked at me, clearly startled. A little thought throbbed in the back of my head – how handsome Aham was, with his broad shoulders and mole-brown eyes, towering over me at six foot five. He was an incredible comedian – insightful and fearless, always one of my favourites – and I'd recently found out he was a jazz musician too, like my dad. (He'd also been divorced multiple times, like my dad, and had two kids and a vasectomy, like my dad when he met my mom.) A mutual friend had mentioned the other day that Aham was a great cook. Was this really a dude I wanted to say 'I might have herpes' to? I shoved the thoughts aside. It's just a skin condition.

'A ton of people in this audience probably have herpes,' I went on, 'but they have to pretend to laugh anyway. That has to be the worst feeling. Why do that to people when you could just write a different joke?'

'I don't know,' he said. 'But you're right. I could have herpes too.'

Aham and I had been chatting at house parties and open-mics for five years, but we didn't really know each other well. Years later, he told me that he'd always been a fan of my writing, but that moment shifted his perception of me forever. 'I was just blown away to hear a woman talk like that,' he said. 'I started to realize that you weren't just funny – I'd always thought you were funny – but that you might be a really, really, radically good person.' Sometimes it pays to tell hot guys you might have herpes, kids!

We were inseparable for the rest of the weekend – we went to an arcade, drank beer, helped Hari come up with burns in a text fight he was having with Marc Maron. Within a year, Aham and I were a couple and he and my dad were playing gigs together.

This was the life I'd dreamed of at twenty-two: hanging out with comics, falling in love, riffing all day. But, in the same moment, I felt my relationship with comedy changing.

# Death Wish

Comedy doesn't just reflect the world, it shapes it. Not in the way that church ladies think heavy metal hypnotizes nerds into doing school shootings, but in the way it's accepted fact that *The Cosby Show* changed America's perception of black families. We don't question the notion that *The Daily Show* had a profound effect on American politics, or that *Ellen* opened Middle America's hearts to dancing lesbians, or that propaganda works and satire is potent and Shakespeare's fools spoke truth to power. So why would we pretend, out of sheer convenience, that stand-up exists in a vacuum? If we acknowledge that it doesn't, then isn't it our responsibility, as artists, to keep an eye on which ideas we choose to dump into the water supply? Art isn't indiscriminate shit-flinging. It's pure communication, crafted with intention and care. Every comedian on every stage is saying what he's saying on purpose. So shouldn't we be welcome to examine that purpose, contextualize it within our culture at large, and critique what we find?

The short answer, I'd discover, is 'nah shut up bitch lol get raped.'

For years, I assumed it was a given that, at any comedy show I attended, I had to grin through a number of brutal jokes about my gender: about beating us, about raping us, about why we deserve it, about ranking us, about fucking us, about not fucking us, about reducing our already dehumanized existence to a handful of insulting stereotypes. This happened all the time, even at supposedly liberal alt shows, even at shows booked by my friends. Misogyny in comedy was banal. Take my wife, please. Here's one I heard at an open-mic: 'Last night I brought this girl home, but she was being really loud during sex, so I told her, "Sssshhh, you don't want to turn this rape into a murder!"' Every time, I'd bite back my discomfort and grin – because, I thought, that's just how we joke. It's 'just comedy'. All my heroes tell me so. This is the price if I want to be in the club. Hey, men pay a price too, don't they? People probably make fun of Eddie Pepitone for being bald.

When a comedian I loved said something that set off alarm bells for me – something racist, sexist, transphobic, or otherwise – I thought: It must be okay, because he says it's okay, and I trust him. I told myself: There must be a secret contract I don't know about, where women, or gay people, or disabled people, or black people agreed that it's cool, that this is how we joke.

But in that moment at the Bridgetown festival, it dawned on me: Who made that rule? Who drew up that contract? I don't remember signing anything, and anyway, it seems less like a universal accord and more like a booby trap that powerful men set up to protect their 'right' to squeeze cheap laughs out of life-ruining horrors – sometimes including literal torture – that they will never experience. Why should I have to sit and cheer through hours of 'edgy' misogyny, 'edgy' racism, 'edgy' rape jokes, just to be included in an industry that belongs to me as much as anyone else?

When I looked at the pantheon of American comedy gods (Bill Hicks, Eddie Murphy, George Carlin, Lenny Bruce, Louis CK, Jon Stewart, Richard Pryor, Chris Rock, Jerry Seinfeld), the alt-comedy demigods (Patton Oswalt, Zach Galifianakis, David Cross, Marc Maron, Dave Attell, Bill Burr), and even that little roster of 2005 Seattle comics I rattled off in the previous chapter, I couldn't escape the question: If that's who drafted our comedy constitution, why should I assume that my best interests are represented? That is a bunch of dudes. Of course there are exceptions – maybe Joan Rivers got to propose a bylaw or two – but you can't tell me there's no gender bias in an industry where 'women aren't funny' is widely accepted as conventional wisdom. I can name hundreds of white male comedians. But how about this: Name twenty female comics. Name twenty black comics. Name twenty gay comics. If you're a comedy nerd, you probably can. That's cool. Now ask your mom to do it.

In the summer of 2012, a comedian named Daniel Tosh was onstage at the Laugh Factory in Hollywood. Tosh is a bro-comedy hero, specializing in 'ironic' bigotry – AIDS, retards, the Holocaust, all with a cherubic, frat-boy smile – the kind of jokes worshipped by teenagers and lazy comics who still think it's cool to fetishize 'offensiveness'. Here's one of Tosh's signature I'm-just-a-bad-baby wape jokes, about playing a prank on his sister: 'I got her so good a few weeks ago – I replaced her pepper spray with silly string. Anyway, that night she got raped, and she called me the next day going, "You son of a bitch! You got me so good! As soon as I started spraying him in the face, I'm like, 'Daniel! This is going to really hurt!'"' See, it's a good one, because being raped really hurts.

This particular night at the Laugh Factory, Tosh was working a bit more meta: according to an audience member who later posted her account anonymously online, he was 'making some very generalizing, declarative statements about rape jokes always being funny, how can a rape joke not be funny, rape is hilarious, etc.' Uncomfortable, the woman heckled: 'Actually, rape jokes are never funny!'

Tosh paused, then addressed the packed house. 'Wouldn't it be funny if that girl got raped by, like, five guys right now? Like right now? What if a bunch of guys just raped her?'

Horrified and frightened, the woman gathered her things and rushed out. She wrote later: 'Having to basic-ally flee while Tosh was enthusing about how hilarious it would be if I was gang-raped in that small, claustropho-bic room was pretty viscerally terrifying and threatening all the same, even if the actual scenario was unlikely to take place. The suggestion of it is violent enough and was meant to put me in my place.'

After the predictable viral backlash, Tosh offered a predictably tepid non-apology, and comedians lined up to support him: Patton Oswalt, Jim Norton, Anthony Jesel-nik, Doug Stanhope. Oswalt wrote, 'Wow, @danieltosh had to apologize to a self-aggrandizing, idiotic blogger. Hope I never have to do that (again).' Stanhope tweeted, '#FuckThatPig.' They were standing up for free speech, for their art. These crazy bitches just didn't get it.

It was a few months into my time at *Jezebel*, and I was tapped to write a response. I felt confident, like I was a good fit for the assignment. I knew I had a more com-prehensive understanding of the mechanics and history of comedy than your average feminist blogger. I'd been writing straight-ahead humour since the beginning of my career – you couldn't say I didn't get jokes. I had enough cred on both sides to bridge the gap between the club and the coven, to produce something constructive. The piece was called 'How to Make a Rape Joke'.

'I actually agree with Daniel Tosh's sentiment in his shitty backpedalling tweet ("The point I was making before I was heckled is there are awful things in the world but you can still make jokes about them #deadbabies"),' I wrote. 'The world is full of terrible things, including rape, and it is okay to joke about them. But the best comics use their art to call bullshit on those terrible parts of life and make them better, not worse.'

Then: 'This fetishization of not censoring yourself, of being an "equal-opportunity offender", is bizarre and bad for comedy. When did "not censoring yourself" become a good thing? We censor ourselves all the time, because we are not entitled, sociopathic fucks... In a way, comedy is censoring yourself – comedy is picking the right words to say to make people laugh. A comic who doesn't censor himself is just a dude yelling. And being an "equal-opportunity offender" – as in, "It's okay, because Daniel Tosh makes fun of ALL people: women, men, AIDS victims, dead babies, gay guys, blah blah blah" – falls apart when you remember (as so many of us are forced to all the time) that all people are not in equal positions of power. "Oh, don't worry – I punch everyone in the face! People, baby ducks, a lion, this Easter Island statue, the ocean..." Okay, well, that baby duck is dead now.'

I analyzed four rape jokes that I thought 'worked' – that targeted rape culture instead of rape victims (in retrospect, I should have been harder on Louis CK, whom I basically let off on a technicality) – and then I explained, 'I'm not saying all of this because I hate comedy – I'm saying it because I love comedy and I want comedy to be accessible to everyone. And right now, comedy as a whole is overtly hostile toward women.'

My point was that what we say affects the world we live in, that words are both a reflection of and a catalyst for the way our society operates. Comedy, in particular, is a tremendously powerful lever of social change. Tina Fey's Sarah Palin impression may have tipped the 2008 election for Obama. Plenty of my peers cite *The Daily Show* as their primary news source. When you talk about rape, I said, you get to decide where you aim: Are you making fun of rapists? Or their victims? Are you making the world better? Or worse? It's not about censorship, it's not about obligation, it's not about forcibly limiting anyone's speech – it's about choice. Who are you? Choose.

I do get it. Tosh plays a character in his act – the charming psychopath. He can say things like 'rape is hilarious' because, according to his defenders, it's obviously not. Because 'everyone hates rape'. It's not an uncommon strain in American comedy: Anthony Jeselnik, Jeff Ross, Lisa Lampanelli, *South Park*'s Cartman. The problem is, for those of us who actually work in anti-rape activism, who move through the world in vulnerable bodies, who spend time online with female avatars, the idea that 'everyone hates rape' is anything but a given. The reason 'ironically' brutal, victim-targeting rape jokes don't work the way Tosh defenders claim they do is because, in the real world, most sexual assault isn't even reported, let alone taken seriously.

Feminists don't single out rape jokes because rape is 'worse' than other crimes – we single them out because we live in a culture that actively strives to shrink the definition of sexual assault; that casts stalking behaviours as romance; blames victims for wearing the wrong clothes, walking through the wrong neighbourhood, or flirting with the wrong person; bends over backwards to excuse boys-will-be-boys misogyny; makes the emotional and social costs of reporting a rape prohibitively high; pretends that false accusations are a more dire problem than actual assaults; elects officials who tell rape victims that their sexual violation was 'God's plan'; and convicts in less than 5 per cent of rape cases that go to trial. Comedians regularly retort that no one complains when they joke about murder or other crimes in their acts, citing that as a double standard. Well, fortunately, there is no cultural narrative casting doubt on the existence and prevalence of murder and pressuring people not to report it.

Maybe we'll start treating rape like other crimes when the justice system does.

No, no one thought that a spontaneous gang rape was

going to take place just then on the stage of the Laugh Factory. But the threat of sexual violence never fully leaves women's peripheral vision. The point of Tosh's 'joke' was to remind that woman that she is vulnerable. More importantly, it reinforces the idea that comedy belongs to men. Therefore, men must be correct when they tell us what comedy is.

There are two competing narratives here. One is the 'Women Aren't Funny' narrative, which posits that women are leading the charge against rape jokes because we are uptight and humourless, we don't understand the mechanics of comedy, and we can't handle being the butt of a joke. Then there's the narrative that I subscribe to, which is 'Holy Shit Women Are Getting Fucking Raped All the Fucking Time, Help Us, Please Help Us, Why Are You All Laughing, for God's Sake, Do Something'. As a woman, I sincerely wish it were the first one.

'How to Make a Rape Joke' wasn't perfect, but it accomplished what I'd hoped: It bridged the gap between feminists and shock comics in a definitive, reasoned way. It went viral like nothing I'd ever written before, the response overwhelmingly supportive from both sides. Many female comedy fans, who'd long been told their voice wasn't welcome in this 'debate', expressed relief. A lot of people said I'd finally shut the lid on the conversation. Even Patton Oswalt retweeted it. The reception was positive enough that I was able to shrug off the relatively small amount of snide abuse from the Tosh faithful:

'*Shut the fuck up Lindy West (who?)*'.

'*Just read @thelindywest's article about Tosh on Jezebel. Two things: 1) Rape is hilarious. 2) I have no idea who she is. Shut the fuck up.*'

'*I hope Lindy and all the people who commented on this article are raped*'

A few characterized my critiques of Tosh as a 'witch hunt', calling me a 'fascist' who was trying to destroy his career and the career of any man who challenged the feminazi orthodoxy. Contrary to their dire warnings, Tosh's popularity soared. As of the writing of this book, he's still on the air.

Overall, I was pleased. It felt like we'd made progress.

A year passed. The following summer, 2013, a feminist writer named Sady Doyle published an open letter to a young comic named Sam Morril. She recently saw him in a show and found his jokes about raping and brutalizing women questionable. Like me the previous year, she hoped to engage him in a constructive dialogue rather than just throwing the same old talking points back and forth.

'One in five women reports being sexually assaulted,' Doyle wrote. 'For women of colour, that number is much higher; one study says that over 50% of young black women are sexually assaulted. (One of your jokes: "I'm attracted to black women. I had sex with one once. The whole time

I was fucking her, she kept using the n-word. Yeah, the whole time, she was yelling NO!") On your Twitter, you warned people that they shouldn't attend one particular set of yours if they'd recently had a miscarriage or been raped. So, like: Are you comfortable excluding that big a chunk of the population from your set?'

Reasonable questions, in my opinion. If you're leveraging people's trauma for laughs, the least you can do is look them in the face. Why make art if you don't have a point of view?

The same week, feminist writer and comedian Molly Knefel published an impassioned essay about the contrast between Patton Oswalt's brutal dismissal of rape joke critiques and his 'too soon' reverence for the victims of the Boston Marathon bombing and the Aurora theater shooting: 'The suffering in Boston, as horrifying as it is, is largely abstract to a nation that has, for the most part, never experienced such a thing. On the other hand, in every room Oswalt performs comedy in, there will be a rape survivor. Statistically speaking, there will be many. There will be even more if he is performing at a university. If exceptional violence illuminates our human capacity for empathy, then structural violence shows the darkness of indifference.'

Both pieces are eminently reasonable and fair – they read beautifully, even years later. The response from comedy fans, however, was horrific. Doyle and Knefel were interlopers, frauds, unfunny cunts, Nazis. Oswalt fans harangued Knefel for days until she took a break from the Internet. Sam Morril eventually replied to Doyle's letter with a lengthy blog post. The key quote? 'Stand-up comedy is a performance, not a discourse.' A dead end. A wall. You are not welcome. Women, it seemed, were obliged to be thick-skinned about their own rapes, while comics remained too thin-skinned to handle even mild criticism.

I was done. I wrote an essay in defense of Knefel and Doyle. It was plainer than 'How to Make a Rape Joke', less affectionately fraternal, less pliant. 'Comedy clubs are an overtly hostile space for women,' I said. 'Even just presuming we can talk about comedy gets women ripped to shreds by territorial dudes desperate to defend their authority over what's funny. "Jokes" about rape and gendered violence are treated like an inevitability instead of a choice; like they're beyond questioning; like they're somehow equally sacred alongside women's actual humanity and physical sanctity. When women complain, however civilly, they're met with condescension, dismissal, and the tacit (or, often, explicit) message that this is not yours, you are not welcome here.'

To my surprise, Oswalt tweeted a link to my post, saying that THIS was feminist discourse he could respect – not like Molly's hit piece. It was a savvy move, to use me for some feminist cred while discrediting the piece that called him out most damningly by name. I replied that if he agreed with me, he agreed with Knefel; our views were not at odds. As we volleyed back and forth, I thought about a night at M Bar in Los Angeles in 2003 or 2004, when I'd shyly approached him after a show and told him he was my favorite comic. He was kind and generous with his time. We talked about Seattle; neither of us could remember the name of the movie theatre on the Ave that wasn't the Neptune. Later, when I remembered, I emailed him: the Varsity. He thanked me, warm and sincere.

Fighting about rape on the Internet was not how I envisioned our next encounter.

I was in a cab to JFK, heading home from a New York business trip, when my friend W. Kamau Bell called my cell. Kamau, at the time, had a weekly show on the FX cable channel, produced by Chris Rock, called *Totally Biased* – a sort of news-of-the-day talk show structured vaguely like *The Daily Show*, but with a social justice bent. Hari wrote for the show; so did Guy Branum. It was a rare writers' room – straight white men were a minority. It was a rare show.

'I want to talk to you about a crazy idea,' Kamau said. 'We want to do a debate about rape jokes, on the show. You versus a comic – it looks like it'll be Jim Norton.'

'Oh, God,' I laughed. 'Do I have to?' Norton is a darling of dark comedy, a prince of the *Opie & Anthony* shock-jock set – a scene that makes Howard Stern look like the World Service.

'Jim's not like a lot of those guys, I promise,' Kamau assured me. 'He's not just like, "Ugh, feminists." You can actually have a conversation with him. We tried to get Colin Quinn, but honestly I think you'll be better off with Jim.'

'Is this a trap?' I said.

'I promise it's not a trap.'

I made arrangements to fly back to New York the following week. Now, the thing about *Totally Biased* was that it was a national television show, and the thing about me was that I was just some fucking lady. Aside from one bizarre time when the Canadian prime-time news had me on to make fun of James Cameron, I think because the anchor had a vendetta, I had never in my life been on television. I didn't have, like, a reel. I wasn't trying to be an actor or a pundit. Me being asked to be on TV was exactly the same as, say, you being asked to be on TV. Or your maths teacher, or your dog, or your mommy. It was bizarre and terrifying, but I agreed, because, hey, maybe I could make a difference. Maybe I could win and comedy would open up just a crack more to female comics and audiences.

My segment was going to be framed as either comedian vs. feminist, or feminism vs. free speech – neither of which, Kamau told me, was his preference, but you had to package things a certain way on television. Fine by me, I said, tamping down my anxiety about debating whether or not it's a good idea to glorify the victimization of women onstage within a framework that explicitly excludes women from even being capable of comedy. What does just some fucking lady know of television?

*Totally Biased* taped in a haunted hotel in Midtown Manhattan – the set a penny-bright, Technicolor diorama, while behind the scenes was this sort of mouldering, dripping, Soviet grey dungeon tower. I gave it fifty-fifty odds that I'd be kidnapped by a masked, erotic ghost on my way to the bathroom. I had a quick sit-down with Kamau and Guy to go over my general talking points. 'The time is going to go faster than you think,' Guy warned me. 'Don't save all your best shit for the end – you won't get to say it.'

Producer Chuck Sklar took me aside and told me that Chris Rock was coming to my taping. 'He doesn't usually come,' he said, 'but he kind of hates this whole rape joke thing. Thinks it's whiny. So he's curious to see how you're going to do.' First of all, solid pep talk, boss. Thanks. Second of all, what the fuck?

One flawed but instructive plank in the debate over rape jokes is the concept of 'punching up' versus 'punching down'. The idea is that people in positions of power should avoid making jokes at the expense of the powerless. That's why, at a company party, the CEO doesn't roast the caretaker ('Isn't it funny how Steve can barely feed his family? This guy knows what I'm talking about!' [points to other caretaker]). Because that would be disgusting, and both caretakers would have to work late to clean up everyone's barf. The issue isn't that it's tasteless and cruel (though it is), but that it mocks the caretakers for getting the short end of an oppressive system that the CEO actively works to keep in place – a system that enables him to be a rich dick.

In a 1991 interview with *People* magazine, journalist Molly Ivins put it perfectly: 'There are two kinds of humour. One kind that makes us chuckle about our foibles and our shared humanity. The other kind holds people up to public contempt and ridicule – that's what I do. Satire is traditionally the weapon of the powerless against the powerful. I only aim at the powerful. When satire is aimed at the powerless, it is not only cruel – it's vulgar.'

Punching up versus punching down isn't a mandate or a hard-and-fast rule or a universal taxonomy – I'm sure any contrarian worth his salt could list exceptions all day – it's simply a reminder that systems of power are always relevant, a helpful thought exercise for people who have trouble grasping why 'bitch' is worse than 'asshole'. It doesn't mean that white people are better than black people, it means that we live in a society that treats white people better than black people, and to pretend that we don't is an act of violence.

Here's the reason I bring this up: I've always been told that 'punching up' was a concept coined by Chris Rock. That attribution might be apocryphal – I can't find a direct quote from Rock himself – but my enduring comedy hero Stewart Lee said it with some authority in a *New Statesman* column about why right-wingers make terrible comedians:

'The African-American stand-up Chris Rock maintained that stand-up comedy should always be punching upwards. It's a heroic little struggle. You can't be a right-wing clown without some character caveat, some vulnerability, some obvious flaw. You're on the right. You've already won. You have no tragedy. You're punching down ... Who could be on a stage, crowing about their victory and ridiculing those less fortunate than them without any sense of irony, shame or self-knowledge? That's not a stand-up comedian. That's just a cunt.'

Are rape jokes so sacred – and misogyny so invisible – that the dude who literally invented the model for social responsibility in comedy can't imagine a world without them? I never got an answer. Rock didn't come to the taping after all.

Backstage, before we got started, I met Jim for the first time – he told me he loved my 'How to Make a Rape Joke' piece, said we agreed more than we disagreed. 'Duh,' I joked. 'I'm right.' We had a good rapport. I felt jumpy but righteous.

When we got onstage, my heart sank quickly. In my intro, to an audience that largely had never heard of me, Kamau explained, 'She's a staff writer for *Jezebel* [who's] called out everyone from Louis CK to Daniel Tosh, and now she's ready to put Jim on blast.' The majority of *Totally Biased* viewers would have no idea who I was, and they heard no mention of my lifelong comedy obsession, the fact that I've done comedy, that I write about comedy, that (at least at the time) I was most widely known in my career for writing humour. They had no reason to assume I had any standing to critique comedy at all.

Before the debate had even started, I was framed as combative, bitchy, shrill. I wasn't there to have a constructive discussion, I was there to put Jim 'on blast'. 'Call-out culture' and putting people 'on blast' are both loaded terms that the anti-social-justice right loves to throw scornfully back at activists. To unfriendly ears – of which, I'd soon learn, there were many pairs listening – the terms connote overreaction, hysteria, stridence. 'Comedian vs. feminist.' I felt uneasy.

Kamau addressed his first question to Jim. 'Jim, do you think comedians should be able to say anything they want to say without any repercussions?'

Silently, I thanked Kamau. Whether intentional or not, the question was framed in a way that forced Jim to concede a few points right off the bat. Everything has repercussions, obviously. The audience laughs, or they don't. They come see you again, or they don't. They buy your album, or they don't. You get booked again, or you don't. He couldn't possibly deny that with a straight face.

Jim nodded enthusiastically, eyes wide. 'If you're trying to be funny, I think! Everybody knows the difference. Reasonable people can sense when you're trying to be funny and when you're trying to be angry. I think, like Matt and Trey said on *South Park*, it's either all okay or none of it's okay.'

He referenced a joke about Hitler that Kamau had

made in an earlier segment, then added: 'If we go down the road of "Hey, don't make fun of this, don't make fun of that," well, then people have a very legitimate argument to go, "Well, don't mention Hitler in any context, because it's never humorous!" So I'm just not comfortable going down that road. I just think as long as you're trying to be funny, you're okay.'

'Everybody knows the difference,' he said. 'Reasonable people can sense when you're trying to be funny.' There's a nasty implication there. The entire rape joke debate can be boiled down to women saying, 'These are not just jokes. These bleed into the world and validate our abusers and reinforce our silence. These are rooted in misogyny, not humour. These are not funny.' Therefore, Jim implied, women are not 'reasonable people'. 'Everybody knows the difference' except feminists, apparently.

Kamau threw the question to me. I breathed sharply through my nose, trying to slow my heart. I wanted to establish myself as someone who wasn't there to equivocate, to bow and scrape, to cede ground to an older, more famous man who talks for a living. I know what I'm talking about, and I mean it. Don't fuck with me. I also wanted to open with a laugh. 'I think that question is dumb,' I said.

'Everything has repercussions. If you're talking about legal repercussions, yeah, I do not think that comedy should be censored, and we're not here to talk about censorship, and' – I gestured to Jim – 'I'm pretty sure we agree.' The censorship argument is a boring red herring – I wanted to knock it down early. Rape joke apologists are quick to cry 'free speech', to use the word 'allowed', as though there are certain things comedians are and aren't 'allowed' to say 'any more'. Barring the most extreme forms of hate speech and credible, specific threats of violence, there is no legislative body governing comedy club stages. The 'thought police' is not a real law enforcement agency.

'What I'm talking about is the kind of repercussion where you choose to say something that traumatizes a person who's already been victimized, and then I choose to call you a dick.'

Jim cut in. 'I totally agree with you...'

(Great. Are we done?)

'...and if you think somebody sucks for what they said onstage, you should blog about it! You should write about it! As long as a person isn't calling for somebody to get in trouble for an opinion or a joke.'

The vagueness of 'trouble' felt like a misdirection. 'But what do you mean by trouble?' I asked, trying to pin him down. 'Is the trouble "people are mad at you"?'

'The trouble is, I do *Opie & Anthony*, the radio show. So a lot of time, the trouble people will do is if you're doing jokes they don't like, they begin to target your advertisers. Because the market should dictate whether or not people enjoy you. But they'll go to the advertisers and say, "They're making jokes that we don't like, so remove your advertising support", which is a way to punish them. That's the type of trouble I'm talking about.'

So Jim was fine with people complaining about comedians, as long as we do it where no one can hear us – as long as we don't complain in any of the ways that actually produce change. No petitions, no letter-writing campaigns, no boycotts. It's odd to invoke 'the market' in such an anti-market sentiment. People boycott because boycotting works – and, more importantly, because it is the only leverage available to us. People target advertisers because they're tired of their hard-won consumer dollars going to pay sexists and racists and homophobes who got those jobs, at least partially, by coasting on the privileges and benefit of the doubt conferred by sexism and racism and homophobia. Also, you know, you're not entitled to a job. It is okay for a white dude to be fired.

It is also okay to draw hard-and-fast distinctions between different ideas – to say that some ideas are good and some ideas are bad. There's a difference between church groups boycotting department store JCPenney because JCPenney put a gay couple in their catalogue and gay people boycotting restaurant chain Chick-fil-a because Chick-fil-a donated millions of dollars to groups working to strip gay people of rights and protections. Gay people wearing shawl-collar half-zip ecru sweaters does not oppress Christians. Christians turning their gay children out on to the streets, keeping gay spouses from sitting at each other's deathbeds, and casting gay people as diseased predators so that it's easier to justify beating and murdering them does oppress gay people.

That said, right-wing Christians should have the right to boycott and write letters to whomever they please. The goal is to change the culture to the point where those boycotts are unsuccessful. You do that by being vocal and uncompromising about which ideas are good and which are bad – which ones we will tolerate, as a society, and which ones we will not. I do not tolerate rape apologia. And, yes, I want to actively work to build a society in which rape apologists face social consequences.

The next few minutes of the debate were more of the same: Kamau asked me if I thought that comedy clubs are 'inherently hostile environments for women', to which I joked, 'Well, they're dark basements full of angry men.' (I took a tremendous amount of abuse for that quip later on, from male comedians who were 'offended' by my characterization of them. Weird – I thought 'reasonable people can sense when you're trying to be funny'.) Jim compared feminists complaining about sexism to religious people complaining about mockery of their religion. He hammered away, yet again, at the idea that 'we all know the difference' between 'a comedy club where you understand that we're trying to have an emotion pulled out of us, which is laughter, and standing up at the office party' – here he pantomimed raising a toast – 'and going, "to rape!"'

I was frustrated. What the fuck is the point of debating

the cultural impact of jokes if your opponent's only argument is 'They're jokes!' It's a cheap trick, forcing me into a position where I have to argue that jokes aren't jokes. So, he's the 'Yay, jokes!' candidate, and I'm the twenty-minutes-of-nuanced-feminist-jargon-that-kind-of-makes-you-feel-guilty candidate.

'I'm sure it's super-comfortable and nice to believe that there aren't systemic forces that are affected by speech,' I said, 'but that's not true, and those of us who are affected by those forces know that's not true. I'm sure sixty years ago there were some "hilarious" jokes about black people, and comedy was way more overtly racist sixty years ago, and it's not a coincidence that life was more hostile and dangerous for black people – not that it's great now, by the way! – and you literally think that's a coincidence? You don't get to say that comedy is this sacred, powerful, vital thing that we have to protect because it's speaking truth to power, blah blah blah, and also be like, "Well, it's just a joke, I mean, language doesn't affect our lives at all, so shut up".'

Jim turned to the audience with a kind, paternalistic smile, as though he felt sorry for me. 'Comedy is not a cause of what happens in society. A lot of times it's a reaction to what's happening and a reflection of what's happening. And comics' speech has never inspired violence.' He then segued into a weird rant against 'the press', who, he said, is 'the only group that I think owes an apology', because they sometimes report on the identities and manifestos of mass shooters, which 'contributes to violence'. Applause.

It was such a transparently irrelevant tangent that I was momentarily speechless. Rape jokes couldn't possibly contribute to the trivialization of rape, because Columbine? It was the rhetorical equivalent of distracting the audience with a squeaky toy. My speechlessness didn't matter, though, because Jim was forging ahead:

'I think the next time somebody walks through a museum and sees a painting that they find highlights or perpetuates a thought that they find objectionable – even a thought that they should find objectionable – then they should take a towel and throw it over the painting. Or I think the next time that person goes to a movie and there's a rape in a movie, they should stand up and hold a board in front of a screen so nobody else can see it. Now, if you did that, people would – what happened to [former NYC mayor] Giuliani when he went after the Brooklyn Museum of Art! People were like, "You fascist! You're going after art for something you don't like!" But if you get mad at a comedian for telling a joke you don't like, people are like, "You go girl." It's either all okay or none of it's okay. I understand why rape is an offensive, awful thing. No one is saying it's not. But sometimes comedy does trivialize what is truly horrible. The roughest set I ever saw a comedian do is Joan Rivers – I saw her at the Cutting Room a few years ago – and I think she's one of the most underrated comics ever [applause] and she did a brutal set. She talked about 9/11, she talked about AIDS, and I mean it was *rough*. And she had zero respect for the boundaries of society. And we all knew why we were there, and we all knew why she was taking everything that hurts us and everything that's sad, and everything that's miserable, and just turning it upside down and looking at it, and we all walked out of there the same as when we walked in. Nobody walked out thinking, "Hey, AIDS is hilarious! AIDS isn't sad and terrible! 9/11 is irrelevant!" We all walked out feeling the same about those subjects, but the relief of comedy is it takes things that aren't funny and it allows us to laugh about them for an hour, and then we have the rest of the day to look at them like they're as horrible and sad as they really are.'

At this point, I had genuinely lost the plot. I stammered and grasped for words. What does Giuliani have to do with rape jokes? How was criticizing comedians on Twitter the same as throwing towels over paintings? Isn't a towel kind of small? Wouldn't a bedsheet do the job better? Also, how many art museums traffic in explicit rape apologia and then brush off any criticism by scoffing, 'Calm down, it's just art'? Again, context matters. Hanging a giant swastika flag in a Holocaust museum, as a historical artefact, is not the same as painting a giant swastika on the wall of the Brooklyn Museum and titling it, 'Kill All Jews'. Culturally, we've evolved to the point where that second piece would never make it into a museum, because we, as a society, have made a decision about which ideas are good and which ideas are bad. We don't have to convene a panel of Holocaust deniers to sign off on that fact in the name of 'free speech'. That's the difference between commenting on rape culture and perpetuating rape culture; choosing to be better, collectively, and caving to the howls of misogynists who insist that sexist abuse is a fair and equal counterpoint to women asking not to be abused.

As for Jim's Joan Rivers anecdote, I'm glad he saw Joan do a great, dark set once. But it's bafflingly presumptuous (and, I'd wager, deliberately disingenuous) to assume that he knew what everyone's opinion on AIDS was when they walked into and out of that theatre. There are plenty of people who consider themselves compassionate, moral, and kind – who have a gay friend and support same-sex marriage – who still, on some level, think of AIDS as a deviant's disease that gay men deserve because of their promiscuity. No, a few off-colour AIDS jokes aren't going to implant prejudice in anyone's brain, but they can damn sure validate and stoke any prejudices that are already lurking.

People like Jim seem to want to believe that the engines of injustice run on outsized hate – stranger rapes in dark alleys, burning crosses and white hoods – but the reality is that indifference, bureaucracy, and closed-door sniggers are far more plentiful fuels.

At the time, the Steubenville rape case had a monopoly on the news – at a high school party in Ohio, two popular football players digitally penetrated an unconscious sixteen-year-old classmate; one also exposed her breasts and put his penis in her mouth. Multiple teenage partygoers took photos and videos of the rape, which they then shared gleefully on social media, accompanied by a proliferation of rape jokes. In another video, friends of the boys reflect on the rape, joking about how 'dead' the victim was. 'She is so raped right now,' one kid says. 'They raped her quicker than Mike Tyson raped that one girl.' The boys' coaches and school administrators attempted to cover up the crime. Media coverage of the investigation and trial repeatedly lamented the loss of the rapists' 'bright futures'. The victim's identity was leaked and her character flayed on live TV.

I practically begged Jim to understand. 'Maybe there's a woman [in the audience] who's wondering whether she should report her rape,' I said, 'and she's sitting there, and everyone's laughing at the idea of how funny rape is, not in a way that is releasing any tension, but in a way that is causing tension, tangibly. Tension that filters out into the world, where we now live in a country where teenage boys think it's totally cool and hilarious to just put their fingers in the vagina of a passed-out child and then videotape it and put it on the Internet.'

Jim cut me off. 'And people reacted appropriately.'

'*Really?*'

'People who saw that were disgusted by that. I'm not talking about the school that covered it up, but the fact that society looked at that and all of us were repulsed by it.'

'All of us were not repulsed by it. No. A lot of people supported those boys.'

Kamau backed me up. 'Have you been on Twitter lately?'

There was the crux. It's easy for Jim and his fans and all the young comedy dudes to pretend like rape culture doesn't exist, because they have the luxury of actively ignoring it. Confronted with a case like Steubenville, he only bothers to look at the parts that reinforce his worldview. He brushed it off with a shrug, because he can, and barrelled on:

'Your Twitter picture is Jeff Goldblum. Jeff Goldblum's first role was a brutal rapist in *Death Wish*. Now I'm not saying anything against Jeff Goldblum, but –'

At this point a producer brought up a screen grab of my Twitter profile – featuring a sweaty Jeff Goldblum in repose, erotically dying from dinosaur bites, in *Jurassic Park* – on the screen behind us. They knew this 'point' was coming. Jim must have told them in his pre-interview. They were prepared.

'– he picked up a blackjack and he said, "you rich C," and he called her the c-word, and they beat her to death in *Death Wish*. Now, we all understand, "Oh, that's an actor doing a role." But why, as an artist, do we give an actor a pass for convincingly playing a brutal rapist, but go after a comedian for making fun of something and mocking something? Like, why do we allow an artist to do something convincingly – what's going to affect a rape victim more? Seeing that rape acted out properly? Or hearing some comedian make fun of it?'

Bad-faith bullshit. Fuck this, I thought. Are you supposed to like and sympathize with Jeff Goldblum's character in *Death Wish*? When people go to watch it, is Jeff Goldblum physically in the room with them pretending to rape people? Does he sometimes break the fourth wall, point into the camera, and say, 'Hey, Karen Ferguson, wouldn't it be hilarious if everyone in this theatre raped you right now?' Why is it a given that seeing a rape acted out is more traumatizing than hearing the concept of rape turned into a joke? Who appointed Jim Norton the arbiter of every rape victim's feelings? If moviegoers just had to deal with the fact that any movie, at any time, could have a random rape scene spliced into it, out of nowhere, that might be a parallel example. A parallel example is not a movie CALLED *Death Wish*, with a rating on it that literally warns you about what's in it, that you've presumably gone to see deliberately because you watched a trailer and decided, 'Yes, this is up my alley.'

For fucking fuck's sake.

'We don't have to choose between those two things,' I said, cold. 'If someone went and saw that movie and they were offended by it, they are more than welcome to complain about it, which is all that I'm doing right now. It's about accountability – if you want to make that product and stand by that, that's fine, but I get to call you a dick, I get to call you out. And if we all agree that it's just a crutch, a hacky premise that people use because you want to get a reaction, you want to shock people, like, why does my vagina have to be your crutch? Can't you use something that's yours? Why do you have to come into my oppression and use me for your closer?'

'I think the best way to end this is for Lindy and I to make out for a while,' Jim joked over Kamau's outtro – deliberately sexualizing me for a laugh at the end of a debate about the dehumanization of women in comedy.

Then it was over. Guy had been right. The time did go too fast, and I didn't get to my best material. I felt pretty good, though. Mostly I just wanted to sleep.

The TV in my hotel room didn't have FX, so I couldn't watch myself. I was grateful.

# It's About Free Speech, It's Not About Hating Women

The first day, it was just a few tweets here and there – regular *Totally Biased* viewers, plus the small number of my fans and Jim's who made it a point to tune in on cable. These broke down pretty uniformly along preexisting ideological lines: Jim's fans thought Jim 'won'; mine sided with me. Everyone seemed to feel that their previously held opinion on rape jokes was validated, and, seemingly, no minds were changed. 'Maybe this'll just be a blip,' I thought as the chatter subsided, honestly a little disappointed. I agreed to do this debate because these ideas are important to me (and, in my opinion, to the development of a more civil, inclusive world) – I wanted to have an impact, maybe shift the conversation, just a hair. I felt good about my performance; I'd held my own against a TV veteran on his turf. You don't go through that much stress to let it just vaporize and blow away.

The second day, my phone buzzed me awake.

*Bzzt.*

*no need for you to worry about rape uggo*

*Bzzt.*

*Jesus Christ this woman is about as fun as dry rape. Lighten up Lindy!*

*Bzzt.*

*you are really annoying. Don't worry no one would ever rape u. Worry about ur Health & the heart attack that's coming #uglycow*

The debate had gone up on YouTube, and Jim had posted it to his social media accounts.

*I love how the Bitch complaining about rape is the exact kind of Bitch that would never be raped. Bitch have you looked in the mirror?*

There were hundreds and hundreds of them. Thousands, maybe. I had never encountered such an unyielding wall of vitriol. They flooded in, on Twitter, Facebook, YouTube, my email, the comments on *Jezebel*.

*Who the fuck, in their right mind, would want to rape you?*

I had been trolled before – for confronting Dan, for mocking men's rights activists, for disliking *Sex and the City 2* – but nothing like this. Nothing could compare to the misogynist rage of male comedy fans at being challenged by an unfuckable woman.

I wanted to rebut every one, but didn't. There was no point. This thing was alive.

*She wants to get screwed so badly I bet you all the rape she is shaking her finger at is exactly what she wants.*

You cannot 'want' rape.

*That big bitch is bitter that no one wants to rape her do some laps lardy holly shit her stomachs were touching the floor*

Rape is not a compliment.

*No one would want to rape that fat, disgusting mess.*

Rape is not a gift or a favour or a validation.

*lets cut the bullshit that broad doesnt have to worry about rape*

Fat women get raped too.

*You're fat, ugly, and unfuckable. You don't have to worry about rape!*

Are you sure?

*There is a group of rapists with over 9000 penises coming for this fat bitch*

There is nothing novel or comedic or righteous about men using the threat of sexual violence to control non-compliant women. This is how society has always functioned. Stay indoors, women. Stay safe. Stay quiet. Stay in the kitchen. Stay pregnant. Stay out of the world. If you want to talk about silencing, censorship, placing limits and consequences on speech, this is what it looks like.

*She won't ever need to worry about rape, ever!*

I don't know any woman who hasn't experienced some level of sexual predation, from catcalls, to unwanted advances at bars, to emotional manipulation, to violent rape. I certainly have – even 'unrapeable' me. All women do need to worry about rape.

*Don't disrespect ppls way of calming themselves down.*
*Embracing the sick idea of rape keeps some from ever*
*actually doing it*

You are a rapist.

*What a fucking cunt. Kill yourself, dumb bitch.*

No.

*Why is it almost all women that hate men are the most*
*un-fuckable people ever.*

I stepped off the plane in Seattle, my phone vibrating
like a pocket full of bees. The local comedy scene had
started in on me at this point: I was a cunt, a fraud, a
failed comic, I knew nothing about comedy and had no
right to comment on it. (Strangely, they'd had boundless
confidence in my expertise back when they were kissing my ass for a mention in the paper.) Someone made
a 'parody' Twitter account called 'Lindy East' (wow, you
guys really are comedy experts), its avatar a stolen photo
of me, my neck and face grotesquely inflated into a massive gullet. One guy – someone I'd never met personally
but who was a regular at the same clubs I frequented –
wrote on Facebook that he wished I'd fall down a flight of
stairs. (Let's call him Dave.) People I knew 'liked' Dave's
comment – one was a regular at The Moth, whom I had

to intro with a smile onstage a few weeks later. But it's just comedy. To worry about my safety was a form of hysteria. Insulting, if you think about it. Can't a nice guy just defend his art?

*Jabba has nothing to worrie about, not even a prison escapee would rape her.*

I was determined to show my face at the open mics that week – to make it clear that I wouldn't be cowed or chased away. 'I'll be at the Underground tonight if anyone wants to talk,' I wrote on Facebook and Twitter. I'd have Aham with me. Nothing would happen. We'd be safe. I hadn't done stand-up in at least a year, so I threw together a few new jokes: 'When people want to insult me, it's always "Jabba the Hutt." Which is really insulting. To Jabba the Hutt. The dude is an intergalactic warlord. He *owns a monster.* I'm a feminist blogger, you guys.'

Aham and I went to the open-mic, did our sets, had fun, and went home.

*There is no way a straight dude would fuck or even rape that ugly heifer. What an annoying cunt.*

Nearly a year later, a mutual friend would show me his text exchange with Dave about that open-mic night.

Unbeknownst to us, Dave was convinced that Aham was going to attack him over his 'fall down the stairs' comment. 'I'm a big boy,' he wrote (sic throughout), 'and I can fight my own battles and take any punches thrown at me but Ill be honest until we squared that away I thought for sure I was going to get in a street fight with that guy. I worked out for two hours just visualizing the fight before the Underground that night, I had a switchblade on me, a 9mm in my trunk and I was ready for anything.'

Dave brought a knife and a gun to a comedy show. Because of a disagreement about whether or not comedy clubs are safe for women. Because the way people talk onstage has no bearing on how they behave in real life.

It's so pathetic, the tough-guy posturing, but so sinister, because, to put it plainly, that's how black men die. Insecure, pee-pants white men assume that any disagreement is a life-threatening situation. Dave assumed Aham was dangerous, and was prepared to shoot him with a gun, even though Dave was the only one in the equation who'd issued a threat of any kind. I've only had a handful of moments like that in my life – where I could see how thin the veil was between my happy, intact world and its complete destruction. How few steps there were between the mundane and the unthinkable. You can see why people stay quiet. Can you see, yet, why I speak up?

*Wouldn't the best ending be that Jim Norton rapes the fat girl.*

Everyone hates rape. Rape is illegal. There is no rape culture. Everyone takes rape seriously. Everyone was horrified by Steubenville. Everyone knows when you're joking and when you're not. Famous men laughing about rape has no effect on the way their fans speak to women they don't like.

My detractors paint me as some out-of-touch idealist, but Jim's the one assuming that all comics approach their art with good intentions – that they're all just trying to make people laugh. That's simply untrue. It's also deeply naive. There's not a single comic working today who's not doing it to fill a personal void; that's why it means so much to them. The idea of someone else laughing is not remotely a good enough payoff to devote your life to something so difficult. Anyway, if Jim's assumptions were true – that comics always have virtuous intentions and people can always tell when someone is joking and when they're not – then we wouldn't be having this discussion.

*Holes like this make me want to commit rape out of anger, I don't even find her attractive, at all, she's a fat idiot, I just want to rape her with a traffic cone*

'Hole' has its own entry on OApedia, a fan wiki page devoted to radio show *Opie & Anthony*: 'Hole is the Opie and Anthony term for the woman who sits in on and ruins most radio shows. The hole opens her mouth saying God-knows-what, adds nothing to the conversation, and chastises the guys for being politically incorrect.' But no, I was told, these people weren't representative of comedians and comedy fans. They were anomalous Internet trolls, and the Internet isn't real life. Except for the guy from real life, the comedian, the one with the gun.

If you've never been on the receiving end of a viral Internet hate mob, it's hard to convey the confluence of galloping adrenaline and roaring dread. It is drowning and falling all at once. In my lowest moment, when it seemed like the onslaught would never stop, an idea unfurled in my mind like some night-blooming flower: They'd handed me a gift, I realized. A suffocating deluge of violent misogyny was how American comedy fans reacted to a woman suggesting that comedy might have a misogyny problem. They'd attempted to demonstrate that comedy, in general, doesn't have issues with women by threatening to rape and kill me, telling me I'm just bitter because I'm too fat to get raped, and suggesting that the debate would have been better if it were just Jim raping me.

Holy shit, I realized. I won.

Their attempts to silence me made my point more effectively than any think piece or flawless debate performance ever could – they were churning out evidence as fast as they could type, hundreds of them working for me, for free. In trying to take down feminism, they turned themselves into an all-volunteer feminist sweatshop. I compiled a sheaf of comments. (They were so uniformly vile I didn't need to dig for the 'worst' ones.) I sat in a big grey easy chair in my living room. Aham filmed me as I read aloud, in one relentless, deadpan beam, staring into the camera for nearly five minutes. Stripping emotion out of such a horror lays the humanity bare: If my feelings are absent, you can't say I'm manipulating you or pushing an agenda. I am a person, and other people said these words to me. They sat down at their computers and chose to type this and send it to another human being. Here is my face. Here are these words. 'It's just the Internet' doesn't seem so true any more.

That video handily exploded myths about me – that I'm working for censorship. That I'm emotionally frail. That I'm against free speech. That I'm afraid of bad words. How could I be? 'I'd like to take a stick and shove it through that mouth of yours and roast you, sexy thing' is hardly going to make it to Thursday nights on prime-time network TV. Show me any joke that's more raw than that video. Show me a comedy routine that takes more risks. If you're so raw. If you're so edgy. Show me.

It worked.

My phone started vibrating for a different reason. The tenor of my Twitter feed had changed. The toilet was swirling the other way, if you will. Every comedian I'd ever loved – even ones who'd dug their heels in on rape jokes the previous summer – threw their support behind me. Joss Whedon got involved. Lena Dunham. It quickly became surreal. The mayor of Seattle tweeted, 'I stand with Lindy West!' Cool, thanks, the mayor.

There was still resistance, but it was sad. You could feel it shaking. Beyond a vocal minority of actual rapists and abusive nihilists, the bulk of my harassers were just bandwagoners trying to impress their comedy heroes. When famous comics realized it was a PR disaster (not to mention a moral one) to align themselves with people who thought 'get raped, piggy' was a constructive avenue of discourse, their ass-kissers had no choice but to follow suit. The tide of public opinion has always turned, invariably, on coolness. People just want to be cool.

Jim, presumably disturbed at the litany of abuse being heaped on me in his name (though still unwilling to admit any connection between misogynist comedy and misogynist comedy fans) wrote an essay for *xoJane*, of all places – the much-derided bastion of teen girl feelings – asking his fans to lay off:

'I am very careful about telling people what they should write or how they should express themselves, but I truly hate a lot of the things that have been directed at Lindy. The anger she's facing is wrong and misguided. If you have a problem with her opinion that's one thing, but to tweet that you hope she gets raped, or that you'd want her to be raped is fucking ignorant.'

What's more, he actually explained the concept of rape culture on *Opie & Anthony*.

'Her point is' – Jim felt around for words that would make sense to this audience – 'uh, the term "rape culture" gets thrown around a lot.'

'Rape culture'. You could hear the snarl of disgust on Opie's face.

Jim cut in, gently contradictory. It's expected of him to pile on – piling on feminists might even be in his contract – but he wouldn't: 'And maybe if someone explains exactly what [rape culture] is, maybe we are...'

After the smallest of pauses, Opie offered, 'A little rapey?'

'Yeah. Possibly.'

You can feel them figuring it out. They reject it immediately, of course, but the spark is there. Two famous white men sniffing imperiously at the existence of rape culture (as though it's theirs to validate or deny) might not seem revolutionary, but to me it was a miracle. Millions of men listen to *Opie & Anthony* – a scene where misogyny isn't just unchecked, it's incentivized – and Jim Norton had not only introduced them to the concept of rape culture, he acknowledged that it could be real. (The question of whether or not Opie and Jim give a shit that our culture might be 'a little rapey' is another matter.) Jim Norton threw rape culture into the fires of Mount Doom. The fires of Mount Doom are still harassing me over rape jokes three years later, but some victories are incremental.

Then, the final nail, Patton Oswalt wrote an open letter about rape jokes on his blog, in which he acknowledged that men might not understand what it's like to be a woman. You can feel the same dawning recognition that Opie and Jim were groping for.

'Just because I find rape disgusting, and have never had that impulse, doesn't mean I can make a leap into the minds of women and dismiss how they feel day to day, moment to moment, in ways both blatant and subtle, from other men, and the way the media represents the world they live in, and from what they hear in songs, see in movies, and witness on stage in a comedy club.'

Just because you haven't personally experienced something doesn't make it not true. What a concept.

And it was over. (Temporarily.) Only the darkest contrarians were willing to posit that Patton Oswalt wasn't a comedy expert. People scrambled to find new trajectories by which their lips could caress his bunghole – suddenly, many open-micers discovered they'd been passionately anti-rape joke all along. Patton was heaped with praise; finally, someone was telling it like it is; he was so, so brave.

I was grateful to him, though it wasn't lost on me and Sady Doyle and Molly Knefel and all the female comics who have been trying to carve out a place for themselves for generations, that he was being lauded for the same ideas that had brought us nothing but abuse. Well, what else is new. Nobody cared about Bill Cosby's accusers – the hordes of women who have accused the veteran comedian of sexual assault – until comedian Hannibal Buress repeated their stories onstage with his veneer of male authority. Regardless, some thirteen-year-old comedy superfan was on his way to becoming a shitty misogynist, but he read

Patton's post, and it might not have changed anything in him right away, but it's going to stick in his head the way things do when you're thirteen. He's going to do what Patton's generation didn't have the guts for. I'll take that victory.

Jim made one throwaway, jokey remark during our debate that's stuck with me more than any other. Referring to comedians milking great material out of life's horrors, he said, 'The worse things are, the better they are for us.' He was being flippant, but it's hardly a rare sentiment among comedians, and it betrays the fundamental disconnect between Jim and me. To Jim, all of life's horrors belong to him, to grind up and burn for his profit and pleasure, whether he's personally experienced said horrors or not. A straight, cisgender, able-bodied white man is the only person on this planet who can travel almost anywhere (and, as the famous Louis CK bit goes, to almost any time in history), unless they're literally dropping into a war zone, and feel fairly comfortable and safe (and, often, in charge). To the rest of us, horrors aren't a thought experiment to be mined – they're horrors.

Bad presidents are a great business opportunity for comedians like Jim. For families trapped in cycles of grinding poverty, bad presidents might mean the difference between electricity and darkness, food or hollow stomachs. Rape means something to me because I've been trapped in a bathroom with a strange drunk man demanding a blow job. Racism means something to my husband because when we drive through Idaho he doesn't want to get out of the car. Misogyny in comedy means something to me because my inbox is full of messages from female comics and comedy writers – some fairly high-profile – who need someplace to pour out their fears and frustrations about their jobs. They can't complain at work; they'll be branded as 'difficult'. They can't complain in public; jobs and bookings are hard to come by as it is. So they talk to me.

If you're a man who works in comedy full-time and you aren't aware of what your female colleagues go through (if you have female colleagues at all), stop assuming that their experience is the same as yours, and start wondering why they aren't talking to you.

The most-viewed segment on *Totally Biased*'s You-Tube channel is a profile of a teenage metal band called Unlocking the Truth, which went viral. At the time of this writing, it has 840,949 views and 1,507 comments. The second-most-viewed clip is an interview with *Daily Show* host Trevor Noah – 612,498 views and 355 comments. My debate with Jim Norton comes in third with 404,791 views.

And 6,745 comments.

Three years later, the thing still gets at least several new comments a week. Honestly, it could be a case study in online misogyny. It has scientific merit. Neither Jim nor I are particularly famous. The debate itself isn't particularly interesting – I mean, it's fine, but it's a niche topic. So what's the draw? The draw is that I'm a disobedient woman. The draw is that I'm fat and I'm speaking authoritatively to a man. The draw is that I've refused to back down even after years of punishment. Nearly every comment includes a derogatory term – cunt, fat, feminazi. Many specifically call out the moment when Jim suggests we make out and I roll my eyes. He was just trying to be funny, they say.

Recently, an *Opie & Anthony* listener started bombarding me with images of mangled bodies, gruesome car accidents, brains split open like ripe fruit. Others cheered him on – high-fiving, escalating, then rehashing it all later in online forums. This cycle isn't some crackpot theory of mine: Misogyny is explicitly, visibly incentivized and rewarded. You can watch it self-perpetuate in front of your eyes. I forwarded the links to Jim and pleaded, 'This is still happening to me. Do you see? How can you not see it?'

His response was terse and firm and invoked Bill Cosby, of all people. The comedy people consume has no bearing on how they behave any more than Bill Cosby's comedy reflected his behavior.

But...Bill Cosby literally joked about drugging and raping women. And, in 'real life', the evidence suggests he drugged and raped women.

Comedy is real life. The Internet is real life. Jim, I realized, doesn't care if his argument is sound – for him, this was never a real debate to begin with. Admitting that I'm right would mean admitting that he's complicit in some truly vile shit. He's planted his flag. He's a wall, not a door.

But comics are a little more careful when they talk

about rape now. Audiences are a little bolder with their groans. It's subtle, but you can feel it. That's where change comes from: these tiny incremental shifts. I'm proud of that. I won. But I also lost a lot.

I can't watch stand-up now – the thought of it floods me with a heavy, panicked dread. There's only so much hostility you can absorb before you internalize the rejection, the message that you are not wanted. My point about rape jokes may have gotten through, but my identity as a funny person – the most important thing in my life – didn't survive. Among a certain subset of comedians and their fans, 'Lindy West' is still shorthand for 'humourless bitch'. I sometimes envy (and, on my bad days, resent) the funny female writers of my generation who never get explicitly political in their work. They're allowed to keep their funny cards; by engaging with comedy, by trying to make it better, I lost mine.

The anti-feminist drumbeat is always the same in these conversations: They're trying to take comedy away from us. Well, Tosh got a second TV show, while the art that used to be my catharsis and my unqualified joy makes me sick now.

The most frustrating thing is that my silly little Autobiography report dreams are finally coming true: I've been offered TV writing gigs, been asked to write pilots, had my work optioned, watched jokes I wrote for other comics get laughs on the air while wannabe open-micers were still calling me 'the anti-comedy' on Twitter. Andy

Richter and his wife Sarah Thyre are friends of mine now. (Coincidentally, he's one of the few big-name comedians who's been tirelessly supportive.) I finally clawed my way to the plateau where my seemingly impossible goals were within reach, and I don't even know if I want them any more.

Video-game critic Leigh Alexander, who is perpetually besieged by male gamers for daring to critique a pastime that is hers as much as theirs, wrote a beautiful meditation on her weariness – on the toll of rocking the boat in an industry you love – for online magazine *Boing Boing*: 'My partner is in games, and his friends, and my guy friends, and they run like founts of tireless enthusiasm and dry humour. I know sometimes my ready temper and my cynicism and the stupid social media rants I can't always manage to stuff down are tiring for them. I want to tell them: It will never be for me like it is for you. This will only ever be joy, for you.'

Men, you will never understand. Women, I hope I helped. Comedy, you broke my heart.

# The Tree

The tree fell on the house when I was sleeping, alone, in the bed that used to be ours, two weeks before my father died, four weeks after Aham told me he was leaving, eight weeks after we moved in together in a new state with grand plans. We shouldn't have gone.

Because even that – 'grand plans' – that's just some nothing I tell myself, still, even now, four years later, when I shouldn't need it any more. It was wrong before we left. It was wrong in the moving truck, it was wrong in my parents' driveway, waving goodbye, my dad wrapped in a plaid blanket and leaning on my mom, probably one of the last times he was out of bed (and I left; I left), it was wrong in Portland, Eugene, Grants Pass, Ashland, Yreka, Weed, Redding, Willows, Stockton, Buttonwillow/McKittrick, and Castaic, and east on the 210 and south on the 2, and off on Colorado, left, right, right, and right.

It was right two months before we moved, at the end of a day with his kids, when we swam in Lake Washington and played his favourite game, 'see who can throw everyone else on the ground first', which he always wins, which is the point, because he is a giant toddler, and we stopped by a garage sale because the sign read 'RARE JAZZ VINYL' and the woman there thought I was the girls' mom – me! – and complimented us on our beautiful children. 'Your mom', she called me, to them. They looked up at me and I panicked, and said, too loud, 'Oh no, I'm not their mom, I'm just SOME LADY!' because I wanted so badly not to fuck this up, not to let him think I was getting any ideas. Don't worry, I'm just some lady. We've only been dating for four months. You just got divorced. I'm not trying to be your family. That would be weird. I know. I'm normal. But.

Then we picked blackberries and made a pie and we swung by my parents' house – it was still my parents' house then, not my mom's house, not truncated and half-empty – and after the kids went inside with the pie he held me back.

'I loved hanging out with you and the girls today,' he said, staring at me with that face.

'I know!' I said.

'I like your parents' place,' he said, looking up at their white Cape Cod-style house blushing in the sunset.

'Me too!' I said.

'What do you think our house is going to be like?' he said.

Meaningful pause.

'In L.A.'

'*Really?* Are you sure?' I jumped up and down, squeezing him.

We weren't moving to L.A. together, we both insisted. We were each independently, coincidentally, moving to L.A. at the same time. He was going to live with some female friend I didn't know; I was going to live with our mutual friend Solomon Georgio. It had to be that way. People didn't move in together after four months. But on that perfect day, heat-drunk and berry-stained and bruised from roughhousing, from playing family, the ruse didn't make sense any more.

We should live together, obviously. We were best friends, and we were in love, even if we didn't say it, and that had to be enough, even though he'd been telling me he was broken since the first night we spent together – broken from abandonment, poverty, kids at nineteen, two divorces by twenty-seven ('that's as bad as being thirteen and a half and divorced once... *times two*,' his bit goes), single fatherhood, depression, a hundred lifetimes of real-ass shit while I was rounding the corner toward thirty still on my mommy and daddy's phone plan. We were friends for eight years before we even kissed. 'Didn't you ever have a crush on me? I'm so handsome,' he asked me later, teasing. 'No. It literally never occurred to me,' I replied, honestly. He was a man. I was still a stupid little girl. Kids? Divorce? That was above my pay grade.

In the summer of 2011, Aham and our friend Solomon were both in the semifinals of NBC's Stand Up for Diversity contest, an annual comedy competition that awards development deals to underrepresented minorities, particularly people of colour. (Every year, some straight white shithead would insist on entering, nobly, in protest, because 'Irish is a minority'.) I'm not sure if the deals ever went anywhere, particularly, but it was a good way to 'get seen' by L.A. industry folks, and it made NBC look progressive.

All three of us were feeling like big fish in those days; we were ready to flop into the L.A. River and see if it'd take us all the way to the sea. (If you know anything about the L.A. River, you know we were screwed from the start.*)

Not to mention the fact that Aham couldn't really move to L.A. anyway. You can't just move when you're an adult man with two kids – he was only going for a few months, six tops, to see if this NBC thing panned out, because you never know, and maybe he'd 'get seen' and become the next David Schwimmer and be able to move out of his three-hundred-square-foot place and he and the girls could have a big new life and no one would have to sleep in the

---

* Every time we drove across a certain bridge, near my sister's house in Silver Lake, Los Angeles, my dad would bring up the great flood of 1938 when the river broke its concrete banks: 'Your grandfather always told me the water came right up level with this bridge. Hoo-wee, boy, all the way up here! Can you imagine?' I couldn't. The L.A. River I knew was a brown, trickling ditch. A joke. Dad was three in 1938, fifteen years before his dad died. My widowed grandmother was so bereft at the loss of her still-young other half that she drank herself into early dementia. She was gone before I was born – it was love that killed her. I'd grind some portent out of that if it wasn't the commonest thing in the world.

laundry room any more. If not, no foul. Nothing to lose. Meanwhile, I was signing a year-long lease in Los Angeles. My love story had a six-month shelf life, at most, in all but the most unlikely circumstances. But I forged ahead. Fuck reality. This was going to be my person. I knew it.

Then, in the driveway, Aham said it out loud – we'd live together, be a real couple – and all of those warnings, overt and covert, that he'd been sending me for the past four months, that he wasn't ready for this, he couldn't do this, his divorce was too recent, their fights were too loud and too mean, his life had too many moving parts, were going to fall away. I had been right to ignore him all along. I knew it. I would make him okay through sheer force of will. He said it. Binding oral contract. Breaking it now wouldn't be *fair*. That's how a little girl thinks. Love was perseverance.

Later, I'd ask him, heaving, 'Why the FUCK would you say that? Why did you trick me? Why did you come here?'

'I just loved you,' he'd say. 'I just wanted to be around you. I told you I couldn't do it. Why didn't you believe me?'

I rented the three of us a little yellow house in Eagle Rock with a big eucalyptus tree in the backyard. The house was owned by a church, which was two doors down, and every so often some church people would come by and try to guilt trip us into coming to one of their 'activities'. The church owned another, identical house next door to ours, where a middle-aged couple lived with their teenage son. The wife, Kathy, had severe early-onset Alzheimer's – she couldn't have been over fifty – and every couple of days she'd wander through our front door, lost and crying. 'Where am I? Where's Jeff? I can't find Jeff!' We'd try to soothe her, walk her home, back into the house that was a dim, dirty funhouse mirror of ours – towels tacked up over the windows, counters piled with fast-food takeout containers, empty of furniture except for a few mattresses on the floor. One particularly sweltering afternoon, trying to get her settled in the back bedroom to wait until her husband got home from work, I realized with a start that he was there, passed out drunk under a pile of blankets. 'Jeff,' I said, shaking him. 'JEFF. JEFF.' He just kept sleeping.

Jeff was a really nice guy. Once, when he came rushing over to collect Kathy from our house, his perpetual cheer slipped for a second and he said, so quietly, 'She used to take care of everything.'

A week before my life broke, I met my sister for coffee and told her that Aham never laughed at my jokes any more.

'Dude,' she said, like it was the most obvious thing in the world, 'don't you know you have to love with an open hand?'

'What?'

Her eyes rolled.

'If you have a bird that you love, and you want the bird to stay and hang out with you and sing for you, you don't clutch it in your fist so it can't get away. You hold your hand out, open, and wait for it to perch there. If you're holding it there, it's not your friend – it's your prisoner. Love with an open hand. DUH.'

'Oh,' I said, stuffing the thought far awa

I didn't see it coming, because I was a

understand what a relationship was – that the

of the thing is two people choosing, every day, to be together,

not one person, drunk on love stories, strangling them both

into a grotesquerie of what she thinks she wants. It didn't

help that the little yellow house next door to Jeff and his

there-but-not-there Kathy was just a few blocks from Occi-

dental, the college campus where, a decade earlier, the cer-

tainty that I was worthless and unlovable had calcified into

a heavy, dragging, extra limb. That was the limb I draped

eagerly around Aham's shoulders, without asking – the

weight that broke his back and pulled us under. It had never

occurred to me that what I needed wasn't to find someone

to help me carry it; what I needed was to amputate.

The descent was swift and boring: I was too much

and too little. He was depressed, distant, and mean. I

pressed myself against him harder, more frantic. His eyes

lost focus; he was always somewhere else. I pressed. He

pulled. I cried every day. He was eliminated from the com-

edy competition. He was angry. On Halloween, he went

to a party. I couldn't come, he said. Sorry. No plus-ones.

He came back at five a.m. We had sex, and then I cried.

'We're going to be okay, right?'

His back was turned.

'No,' he said, and everything changed. 'I don't think

we're going to be okay.'

I had been sad before. I had been very sad. This was

something new. I felt liquefied. Even writing this, years later, I'm sobbing like he's dead.

I had waited so long for someone to pick me. And then he changed his mind.

I went across town to my friends Ella and Owen's house for a few weeks, and they let me sit on their couch all day and stare and cry; Ella made me a therapy appointment and tried to get me to eat; Owen made me laugh by narrating elaborate parlour dramas between their three enormous, idiot dogs; at night, the dogs would forget who I was and trap me in the bathroom, barking wildly, until someone got up and rescued me.

I wrote Aham a long, impassioned email, like a teenager – the gist of which was, 'I don't understand. We love each other. It's enough.'

He wrote back, in short, 'You're right. You *don't* understand. It's not.'

I drove him to the airport and he chattered the whole way about a radio show that was going to produce one of his stories; he thought we were just going to be friends now. He thought I knew how to compartmentalize, like he did. 'I've missed talking to you so much,' he said, beaming. I watched him blankly. He was going back to Seattle for Thanksgiving; I was going too, the next day.

That afternoon, I noticed a weird charge on my bank statement. Someone had stolen one of my chequebooks – I must have dropped it – and written a $750 cheque to herself. I called the bank's fraud department; they said they would take care of it. I woke up the next morning with a balance of minus $900,000. Apparently, that's the policy when someone reports cheque fraud to Bank of America; the bank subtracts $900,000 from their balance to preclude any further fraudulent withdrawals.*

I was a negative-millionaire. I shrugged and flew home to Seattle.†

At Thanksgiving dinner, we ate mashed potatoes and bad stuffing from the grocery store deli counter down the street. My dad threw up at the table and then started to cry. Aham called me to tell me about something goofy his mom had done to the turkey. I approximated a laugh. Downstairs, I took off my clothes and shambled toward bed. A massive period clot fell, *right out of me*, like a crimson water balloon, on to my mom's white carpet. I looked at it and got in bed.

The plane shook and lurched in the Santa Ana winds, but we returned to Burbank without particular trouble. I took a cab home. Solomon was out of town. Aham was still in Seattle. The wind picked up. The power went out. The windows rattled. I took a sleeping pill and curled into a ball and tried to hide from the dark and the wind in the bed that had been

---

* Yo! Bank! Other policy suggestion! TELL PEOPLE ABOUT THE MINUS-A-MILLION-DOLLARS POLICY BEFORE YOU MINUS-A-MILLION-DOLLARS THEM RIGHT WHEN THEIR DAD IS DYING AND THEIR PERSON JUST CHANGED HIS MIND.

† The bank eventually refunded my $750 and said I could decide whether or not to file a police report. I didn't. I'm glad that lady got to keep that money – I hope it helped her out of a jam.

ours, the first bed I'd ever shared with someone who loved me and picked me and then changed his mind. At a certain point, a groaning started, then a cracking, then a pounding. It sounded like enormous beasts were hurling themselves against the house. Nothing had ever been louder. Growing up, I'd had a recurring nightmare about a flood, where the water rose right up to the level of my bedroom window, and animals – monstrous hippos, rampaging elephants – would lunge out of the storm, smashing their bulk against the glass. It must be the sleeping pill, I thought. A nightmare bleeding into real life. It sounded like the walls were coming down around me, like something was prying away the roof. I took another sleeping pill and shook.

I woke up in the morning embarrassed at my hallucination. It was just a storm. Was I really so pathetic? I walked into the kitchen.

The world was gone. Everything was leaves. Leaves pressed up against every window, through the screens, over the sills. The glass back door was a wall of leaves, Solomon's room was leaves, leaves, leaves. Someone banged on the door. I jumped.

The Santa Anas had been too much for the old eucalyptus tree; it had keened and struggled as I half slept, eventually cracking right in half and crushing our little yellow house. The little house that was supposed to be our love story. It's a metaphor you couldn't use in fiction. Too on the nose. Any good editor would kill it, and probably fire you.

My mom called. She was crying. It was time. I went back to the airport.

# The End

Until I watched a death up close, I always felt avoidant around grief and grieving people. It was one of the things I hated most about myself – my complete loss of social fluidity among the heartbroken – though I know it's common. I am a shy person at heart, and a grieving acquaintance is a shy person's nightmare: The pressure to know the 'right' thing to say. Seeing a person without their shell. The sudden plunge, several layers deeper than you've ever been, into someone's self, feigning ease in there so you don't make them uneasy. Navigating, by instinct, how much space you should be taking up – or, even worse, bringing yourself to ask.

I spent a lot of time alone as a kid. I've never been an easy hugger. The social conventions that keep human beings separate and discrete – boundaries, etiquette, privacy, personal space – have always been a great well of safety to me. I am a rule follower. I like choosing whom I let in close. The emotional state of emergency following a death necessarily breaks those conventions down, and, unfortunately, I am bad at being human without them.

I never caved to the impulse, of course – it's repulsively selfish and I've chewed my cheek bloody just admitting it here. Other people's grief is not about you; letting self-consciousness supersede empathy is barbaric. I'm the first to drop off a casserole, send flowers and a card. 'Anything I can do.' 'Thinking of you so much right now.' But before death had ever touched me directly, those interactions felt like trying to dance, sober, in a brightly lit room.

Someone picked me up at the airport and drove me to my parents' house, where my dad either was or wasn't, I can't remember. He was in and out of the hospital so often at that time it was hard to keep track, elation swapping places with despair at flickering speeds like a zoetrope animating the last days of my childhood. Flick, flick, flick.

Even though my mother was a nurse and I grew up immersed in hospital culture – talking eyeball surgery over dinner, specimen cups full of mandarin oranges in my school lunch – I didn't understand shit about hospitals. I didn't know that even the best ones were miserable and lonely places where you couldn't sleep more than a couple of hours at a stretch; where, with each second you weren't discharged, you could see the outline of your death shiver into focus. Hospitals were full of medicines and machines and doctors and hyper-competent people like my mother. I thought they were a place you went to get better, not a place you went to die.

Cancer doesn't hand you an itinerary. It's not like, up to a certain point, you have an okay amount of cancer, and then one day the doctor's like, 'Uh-oh! Too much cancer!' and then all your loved ones rush to your bedside for some stoic, wise goodbyes. Cancer, at least in my dad's case, is a complex breaking down of multiple systems, both slow and sudden. You have six months and then you have six hours. Treatments are messy, painful, and often humiliating. The cost/benefit is anything but clear.

My dad didn't want to die. He turned seventy-six that year, but until his prostate fucked everything up, he radiated the same tireless exuberance as he always had. My mom said he didn't like hearing his own prognoses, so she met with the doctors herself, carried the future inside her all alone. She, the realist, and he, the fantasist, as ever.

In those final weeks, though, even Dad couldn't deny that his body was failing. That horrible Thanksgiving, when he vomited into the empty margarine tub at the dinner table, was when I first noticed it. He had begun grieving – for himself, for the life he wasn't ready to leave behind. I, true to form, was terrified of his grief.

Those days eat at me. Why didn't I spend more time sitting with him? Why did I sleep so much? Why didn't I read out loud to him, our favourite books, the ones he read to me when I was little? Why was I so fucking chirpy in all of our interactions, desperate to gloss over the truth, instead of letting myself be vulnerable with him? Why the fuck did I move to L.A. three months before he died? What was wrong with me? Who does that?

He wanted me to go, though. That was before he admitted he was dying – if I had stayed, it would have been confirmation that something was really wrong – and there was nothing he loved more than watching his children stride out into the world and flourish. 'Knock 'em dead, kid,' he said. And I did. It's so fucking unfair that he didn't get to see it.

Eventually, I ran out of chances to sit with him, to be vulnerable, to tell the truth. We went to the hospital for the last time.

As Dad drifted in and out of consciousness, my sister and I read to him from the book he was halfway through at the time: *A Jazz Odyssey: The Life of Oscar Peterson*. Aham once told me that Oscar Peterson, my dad's hero, was the lovable dork of the jazz pantheon. 'He's incredibly well respected,' Aham hedged. 'He's amazing – just the least edgy player ever. He's kind of like Superman.' Peterson never had a drug problem; he loved his wives; he was huge in Canada. Unsurprisingly, then, where my sister and I picked up in *A Jazz Odyssey*, Peterson was describing a hobby that I can confidently declare the exact opposite of being a philandering New York needle junkie: pottering around America's parks and monuments with his wife Kelly in their brand-new Winnebago.

My dad roused every once in a while and chuckled as Peterson detailed with reverence the Winnebago's gleaming chrome accents and spacious over-cab loft bed. The open road, the great plains, Kelly by his side – this was the life. Until it came time to empty the Winnebago's sewage tank. Oscar was pretty sure he could figure it out unassisted.

I looked up from the book, into my sister's expectant face and over at my dad's unconscious one. Was Oscar Peterson about to tell us a story about gallons and gallons of his and his wife's liquefied faeces spraying out of a Winnebago? Was I about to read it out loud, in a soothing voice, at my father's deathbed? Yes. Yes, I was.

Dad's hospital room was small – only two guests could hang out in there comfortably – so my mom, my sister, and I took turns sleeping in the chair next to his bed, holding his hand, while one of us lounged on the cushioned bench under the window and the odd woman out decamped to the cafeteria or the 'family lounge' down the hall. The family lounge was a small, windowless room with an old TV, a couch upholstered in what looked like leftover airport carpet, and a pile of battered, cast-off VHS tapes, because nothing takes the edge off your father's slow suffocation like *Speed 2: Cruise Control*.

Did you know that sometimes there just isn't anything else that doctors can do to save your dad? I knew it intellectually, before this experience, but I didn't understand it in practice. In practice, it means that, at a certain point, a fallible human being called a doctor has to make a subjective decision that it is no longer feasible to mitigate both the internal bleeding and concomitant dehydration of your father, so all you can do is give him enough morphine that it doesn't hurt so much when he drowns inside of his own body. And you have to go, 'Okay,' and then let them do that. And then wait.

My dad lost consciousness on Saturday night. My mom told me to go home and sleep, that she'd call me if it looked like he was going to go. I passed out on my parents' couch, making peace with the fact that I would probably miss the end. It was okay. I had said goodbye, told him I loved him. But the next morning, when I woke up, he was still holding on (he was always strong, he didn't want to go), so back I went. We picked up our routine again – chair, bench, family lounge – and we sat there. Waiting. All day Sunday, into Monday. Each breath got slower and rougher – I use a cafetière now because I can't bear the percolator – and we sat and listened to every one.

Sometimes a team of doctors would come in and loom over us with well-rehearsed but clinical concern. 'How are you doing?' they would ask. Oh, you mean besides sitting here on this plastic hospital chair listening to the world's best dude struggle for breath for the past thirty-six hours? Um, fucking gangbusters, I guess. 'Is there anything we can do?' Apparently not, considering this whole long-slow-death thing that's happening in this room right now. Also, you're the doctor. You tell me.

I have never wanted anything as much as I wanted

that shitty purgatory to be over. Except for one thing –
which was for that shitty purgatory to never be over.
Because when it's over, it's over. And eventually it was.
Monday afternoon, my dad stopped breathing, faded to
black-and-white like an old movie, and – I don't know how
else to describe it – flattened slightly, as though whatever
force was keeping him in three dimensions had abruptly
packed up and moved on. He was, and then he wasn't.
One moment his body was the locus of his personhood,
the next moment our memories had to pick up the slack.

A nurse brought us granola bars and juice cartons on a
little rolling trolley, like a 'your dad died' door prize. A guy
with a mop came in to start cleaning up the room for the
next patient. There was someone with a clipboard, asking
questions. 'Could you give us a fucking minute?' my mom
snapped. 'My husband just died thirty seconds ago.'

We sat with the body that used to be him. I didn't
understand the point, honestly.

Back in November, before Thanksgiving, before the tree
fell on the house, before the hospital, Aham and I met up
at a bar on Seattle's Capitol Hill. We hadn't spoken in a
week or so, and my pain and anger had cooled to something more permeable. I'd spent that time with friends
and family, eating and drinking and carrying on, coming
back to myself – getting reacquainted with the person I'd
been before Aham, even before Mike. I had an identity

other than my relationship – I remembered it now – and this grimy fish tank I built around us hadn't been good for me either.

Grudgingly, I'd come to see Aham's point a little bit. He fell in love with *this* person, and in my desperation to hang on to him, I morphed myself into something else entirely. He wanted a partner but I gave him a parasitic twin. Except worse than that. A parasitic twin that cried all the time. Worst *X-Files* episode ever.

At the bar, Aham and I ate fries and got drunk. We didn't talk about our relationship and I didn't cry. I felt detached; my capacity for sadness was maxed out. I had given up on trying to force him to come back to me, and he apologized for trying to force me to be his friend. Somehow, we had fun. Relief poured back and forth between us, quietly electric. Aham had a gleam I hadn't seen in months. For a minute, we held hands, and something woke, tiny but palpable, in my chest. Outside, it snowed, big, fat, wet flakes. I dropped him at the bus stop and said I'd see him in L.A., feeling something that wasn't quite despair for the first time in a month. He said we'd talk. Of course, that never happened – he flew back down the day after the tree fell, and I was already gone.

I took my bereavement juice carton to the family lounge and called Aham in L.A.

'Can you just come?' I sobbed.

'Of course,' he said.

We weren't back together, but we weren't not together. We weren't sleeping together, but he slept in the bed with me and held on to me as much as I needed. He ran errands for my mom, made her laugh, cooked eggs Benedict, booked a piano player for the funeral, figured out how to get a banquet licence while I cried in the liquor store. My aunt and uncle came up from Arizona and stayed with us; Aham's girls would come on the weekends; friends and family dropped by nearly every day. We sat around and drank beer and watched football, all piled together in that little white house. It was a beautiful chaos, the same kind my mom grew up in and loved so much, the kind that I never understood growing up alone. It's weird to look back at the saddest month of my life and see that little vein of joy.

Aham and I weren't getting back together – we swore we weren't, we couldn't – but when I wasn't looking, he had become my family anyway.

# The Beginning

We went back to L.A. and lived in limbo for a few months. Aham went on tour; I started working at *Jezebel*. We weren't 'together', but we were happy in a totally unfamiliar way.

I'm not saying that if your relationship is in trouble you should cross your fingers that your dad dies.* But after my dad's funeral, I was older. Aham wasn't the only thing in my world any more. My pain (and, later, my career) had pushed him aside a little bit, and that space was exactly what he needed. 'I am a narcissist,' he jokes, 'but I didn't actually want to date my own reflection.' Aham had come

---

* Unless you hate your dad, I guess, in which case you can cross your fingers for whatever you want, *as long as you are not crossing them around the trigger of a dad-murdering gun!!!* (Look. Don't murder your dad. It will not make your boyfriend get back together with you. I DON'T KNOW HOW MUCH MORE CLEARLY I CAN SAY THIS.)

through for me, in that month of emotional triage, with a selflessness that I think surprised us both – not out of some sense of obligation, but because he really wanted to be there, in my mom's basement, mixing gin and tonics for my auntie Astri.

It was a horrendous period, but somehow we had fun. We worked so hard to make each other laugh. We were just ourselves again. It was like a reset.

When Aham got back from tour, we sat down for a two-day feelings marathon. Even for me, a professional leaking sad-bag, it was a nightmare. There were scheduled breaks. We punched in and out like trudging coal miners. We wrote up a contract specifying how much crying was allowed. (My opening offer was '100 per cent of the time'; Aham low-balled with a blank stare.) The details are boring, and some of them are just mine, but at the end of it, we were a couple again. I don't even think of it as 'getting back together', because it didn't feel like a reconvening of the old relationship – it was a new one.

'If we're going to do this,' he told me, giving me his most Intense Face, 'we're really doing it. Don't change your mind on me.'

It's hard to talk about, because the realist in me (i.e., my mom) kind of doesn't believe that 'couples getting back together' is a real thing. It's something I believed in when I was a child, when I understood a relationship as something that happened to you, not something you built, and I thought *The Parent Trap* was the ultimate love story. But we really did do it, and the only explanation I can offer is that we weren't the same people in Relationship: Part Deux as we were in Relationship: The Phantom Menace.

Aham still wasn't sure that he believed in marriage any more. It was understandable – he'd been divorced twice in the previous six years. I used up some of my tear allotment on that, not because I have any particular attachment to the institution of marriage, but because I just wanted to prove to the world that I was worth marrying. I grew up assuming that I would never get married, because marriage was for thin women, the kind of women who deserved to be collected. How could I be a bride when I was already what men most feared their wives would become? I was the *mise en place* for a midlife crisis. I was the Ghost of Adultery Future. At least, that's what I'd been taught. Aham was my shot at vindication. Come on, man. Think of all the fat girls we can inspire with our lifelong legal commitment!

'Okay, what if we still like each other this much in five years?' I bargained, annoyingly persistent *but in a charming way, I'm sure*. 'Can we talk about getting married then?'

'In five years, if we still like each other exactly this much, sure, we can *talk* about getting married,' Aham said, rolling his eyes. 'You are the most annoying person on earth.' That was good enough for me. It was basically a proposal.

We moved back to Seattle a few weeks after that. We rented a house and settled into a routine, our pre-breakup life already distant and foreign, like it happened to someone else. Every day I take his face in my hands and squeeze, because I think he might be a mirage; he declares 'Crab Fingers', his second-favourite game, and pinches me until I fall out of bed. I call him and say gross stuff like, 'I want to hug you and kiss you!' and he goes, 'Who is this? Jessynthia?' and pretends to have a secret family. We show our love in different ways. But being in love holds its own kind of challenges.

Once, Aham and I were sitting at a bar, holding hands, and a woman recognized me. She was a fan of my writing, so she came up to introduce herself, and we shambled through a few minutes of pleasant chitchat. Sensing the conversation was running out of steam, she asked me one of the questions that people always ask me in those awkward, floundering moments: 'So, what's it like to work from home? Aren't you lonely?'

'Not really,' I said. I gestured to Aham. 'He works from home, too. It's hard to feel alone when there's a guy constantly playing the trumpet in your face.'

She laughed and turned to him. 'So, you two are roommates?'

Yes, lady. We are platonic adult roommates who hold hands at bars. This is, clearly, the only logical explanation. Actually, since you asked, I recently sustained a pulsing gash to the palm and he's just holding the wound closed until paramedics arrive. Also, every night before bed, a rattlesnake bites me on the mouth and he has to suck out the poison. It's the weirdest thing. We should probably move.

I wasn't surprised that this woman took so many wilful leaps past 'couple' and landed on 'roommates' in her split-second sussing-out of our relationship – it happens all the time. But it was a disheartening reminder of an assumption that has circumscribed my life: Couples ought to 'match', Aham and I do not. I am fat and he is not. He is conventionally desirable and I am a 'before' picture in an ad for liquefied bee eggs that you spray on your food to 'tell cravings to buzz off'! (COPYRIGHTED. SEND ME ALL THE MONEY.) It is considered highly unlikely – borderline inconceivable – that he would choose to be with me in a culture where men are urged to perpetually 'upgrade' to the 'hottest' woman within reach, not only for their own supposed gratification but also to impress and compete with other men. It is women's job to be decorative (within a very narrow set of parameters) and it is men's job to collect them. My relationship throws off both sides of that equation, and a lot of people find it bewildering at best, enraging at worst.

There are long, manic message board threads devoted to comparing photos of me with photos of Aham's thin, conventionally pretty second ex-wife (number one is blessedly absent from the old MySpace page he doesn't know how to take down; number two is not so lucky), and dissecting what personality disorder could possibly have caused him to downgrade so egregiously. Waiters always assume we want to split the bill. Women hit on him right in front of me – and the late-night Facebook messages are a constant – as though they could just 'have' him and he would say, 'Oh, thank God you finally showed up,' and leave me, and some dire cosmic imbalance would be corrected. It's nothing personal, it's just that they 'match'. They can talk about hot-people problems together – like 'too many clothing options' and 'haters.' I wouldn't understand.

It's not that I'm not attracted to fat men – I've dated men of all sizes – but the assumption that fat people should only be with fat people is dehumanizing. It assumes that we are nothing but bodies. Well, sorry. I am a human and I would like to be with the human I like the best. He happens to not be fat, but if he were, I would love him just the same. Isn't that the whole point? To be more than just bodies?

When I think back on my teenage self, what I really needed to hear wasn't that someone might love me one day if I lost enough weight to qualify as human – it was that I was worthy of love now, just as I was. Being fat and happy and in love is still a radical act. That's why a wedding mattered to me. Not because of a dress or a diamond or a cake or a blender. (Okay, maybe a cake.*)

Aham took me out for dinner on my thirty-second birthday, then suggested a 'quick nightcap' at our neighbourhood bar. Everyone was there – it was a surprise – our friends, our families, the kids, a cake. I was so happy.

---

* We had like six.

Aham took my hand and led me to the back; there was a paper banner that said my name (the bartender made it – we go there a lot); our friends Evan and Sam were playing a duet on cello and bass. I was confused. Why were there sombre strings at my birthday party? Why was Aham doing Intense Face? Wait, it's almost ten p.m. on a school night and we're at a bar – why ARE the kids here? Then it all happened at once: the knee, the ring, the speech, the question, the tears. All the hits. It was a full-blown grand gesture.

He tricked me! He said five years. I was ready to wait five years. He only lasted two.

Later, I asked him why he did it that way – such a big spectacle, such an event, not precisely our style – and I expected something cliché but sweet, like, 'I wanted to make sure our community was a part of our marriage', or, 'I wanted everyone to know how much I love you'. Instead, he said, 'One time when you were drunk you told me, "If you ever propose to me, don't do it in the bullshit way that dudes usually treat fat girls. Like it's a secret, or you're just trying to keep me from leaving you. Thin girls get public proposals, like those dudes are winning a fucking prize. Fat chicks deserve that, too."'

It's not that I'd ever particularly yearned for a grand gesture – the relationship I cherish lives in our tiny private moments – but the older I get and the longer I live in a fat body, the harder it is to depoliticize even simple acts. A public proposal to a publicly valued body might be personally significant, but culturally it shifts nothing. A public proposal to a publicly reviled body is a political statement.

As soon as you start making wedding plans, you're bombarded with (among a million other beckoning money pits) a barrage of pre-wedding weight-loss programs. Because you're supposed to be as thin as possible on your special day. After all, there will be pictures! And what if someone remembers your butt as looking like what your butt looks like?! 'I'm only eating grapefruit and steam until my wedding.' 'I enrolled my whole wedding party in bridal boot camp.' 'I bought my dress in a size 4 even though I'm a size 6.' And that's totally fine, of course, if that's your priority. It wasn't mine.

I don't hide any more in my everyday life, and I definitely wasn't going to hide at my wedding.

We got married a year and a half after the proposal, in July, at my parents' cabin a few hours outside of Seattle. Even though I believe that death is a hard return, I can always feel my dad at the cabin. It was his favourite place. I walked down the aisle to a recording of him playing 'Someone to Watch Over Me' on the piano; Aham wore a blue plaid suit; a bald eagle flapped over the ceremony; someone spilled red wine on one of the beds and my mom was in a good enough mood to forgive them; I got my fucking period (will you never *leave me be*, fell ghoul?!); it poured down rain after a month of uninterrupted sunshine, then abruptly stopped just as we emerged from the tent to dance; Meagan killed everyone with a toast about how Great-Aunt Eleanor died believing Meagan and I were lesbian lovers; a friend of mine, post-late-night-hot-tubbing, got confused about the route to the bathroom and walked into my mom's bedroom naked. Oh, and Aham's one-hundred-year-old great-grandmother had a stroke on the way to the wedding, went to the hospital, got better, *and still came and partied*. It was a gorgeous, chaotic, loving, perfect day.

We scribbled our vows five minutes before the ceremony.

Aham's read:

> *You know that thing that I do that you hate? That thing where I talk about how years ago when we were friends and I always wanted to hang out with you and I would always text you, and I would see you and be like, 'We should hang out!' and then you'd always cancel on me? I'm never going to stop bringing that thing up, because I like being right. And all those times that I tried so hard to get you to hang out with me, and I just wanted to be around you so much, I've never been more right about anything in my life. The only way I can think to say it is that you are better than I thought people could be.*

I am happier than I thought people could be.

# Slaying the Troll

One ordinary midsummer afternoon in 2013, I got a message from my dead dad. I don't remember what it said, exactly, and I didn't keep a copy for my scrapbook, but it was mean. My dad was never mean. It couldn't really be from him. Also, he was dead – just eighteen months earlier, I'd watched him turn grey and drown in his own magnificent lungs, so I was like 80 per cent sure – and I don't believe in heaven, and even if I did I'd hope to nonexistent-God they don't have fucking Twitter there. It's heaven! Go play chocolate badminton on a cloud with Jerry Orbach and your childhood cat.

But there it was. This message.

It was well into the Rape Joke Summer and my armour was thick. I was eating thirty rape threats for breakfast at that point (or, more accurately, 'you're fatter than the girls I usually rape' threats), and I felt fortified and righteous. No one could touch me any more. There was nothing remarkable about this particular tweet – oh, some white dude thinks I'm ugly/fat/stupid/humourless/boring? Does the Pope fart in Latin? – and by all conceivable logic it shouldn't have even registered. It certainly shouldn't have hurt.

The account was called 'Paw West Donezo' (Paw West because his name was Paul West, and donezo because he was done being alive, done making up funny songs, done doing crossword puzzles, done not being able to get the printer to work, done getting annoyingly obsessed with certain kinds of ice pops, done being so strong, done being my dad).

'Embarrassed father of an idiot,' the bio read. 'Other two kids are fine though.'

His location: 'Dirt hole in Seattle.'

The profile photo was a familiar picture of him. He's sitting at his piano, smiling, in the living room of the house where I grew up. Some of the keys on that piano still have grey smudges worked into the grain, the ghost of old graphite where he'd pencilled in the names of the notes for me when I was small. I never practised enough; he always pretended not to be disappointed. The day they sold that house, when I was twenty-five, I sat on the stairs and sobbed harder than I ever had, because a place is kind of like a person, you know? It felt like a death, I thought. My family was broken, I thought. I wouldn't cry that hard again until December 12, 2011, when I learned that a place is not like a person at all. Only a person is a person. Only a death is really a death.

Watching someone die in real life isn't like in the

movies, because you can't make a movie that's four days long where the entire 'plot' is just three women crying and eating candy while a brusque nurse absentmindedly adjusts a catheter bag and tries to comfort them with cups of room-temperature water.

Saturday afternoon, when we could feel his lucidity slipping, we called my brother in Boston. My dad's first-born. 'You were such a special little boy,' he said. 'I love you very much.' He didn't say very many things after that.

I would give anything for one more sentence. I would give anything for 140 more characters.

The person who made the 'Paw West Donezo' account clearly put some time into it. He researched my father and my family. He found out his name, and then he figured out which Paul West he was among all the thousands of Paul Wests on the Internet. He must have read the obituary, which I wrote two days after my dad's lungs finally gave out. He knew that Dad died of prostate cancer and that he was treated at Seattle Cancer Care Alliance. He knew that I have a brother and a sister. And if he knew all that, he must have known how recently we lost him.

My armour wasn't strong enough for that.

What was my recourse? What could I do? This was before Twitter had a 'report' function (which, as far as I can tell, is just a pretty placebo anyway), and it's not illegal to reach elbow-deep into someone's safest, sweetest memories and touch them and twist them and weaponize them to impress the ghost of Lenny Bruce or what-the-fuck-ever.

Hell, not only is it not illegal, I'm told it's a victory for free speech and liberty. It's just how the Internet works. It's natural. It's inevitable. Grow a thicker skin, piggy.

'Location: Dirt hole in Seattle.'

All I could do was ignore it. Hit 'block' and move on, knowing that that account was still out there, hidden behind a few gossamer lines of code. 'Paw West Donezo' was still putting words in my dead father's mouth, still touching his memory, still parading his corpse around like a puppet to punish me for…something. I didn't even know what.

I'm supposed to feel okay just because I can't see it?

Yes. You're supposed to feel okay just because you can't see it. There's no other way, we're told. We couldn't possibly change the culture, we're told.

There's no 'winning' when it comes to dealing with Internet trolls. Conventional wisdom says, 'Don't engage. It's what they want.' Is it? Are you sure our silence isn't what they want? Are you sure they care what we do at all? From where I'm sitting, if I respond, I'm a sucker for taking the bait. If I don't respond, I'm a punching bag. I'm the idiot daughter of an embarrassed dead guy. On the record. Forever.

Faced with a lose-lose like that, what do you do? Ignoring 'Paw West Donezo' wasn't going to chasten him, or make me feel better, or bring my dad back.

So I talked back. I talked back because my mental health – not some troll's personal satisfaction – is my priority. I talked back because it emboldens other women to talk back online and in real life, and I talked back because women have told me that my responses give them a script for dealing with monsters in their own lives. Most importantly, I talked back because Internet trolls are not, in fact, monsters. They are human beings who've lost their way, and they just want other people to flounder too – and I don't believe that their attempts to dehumanize me can be counteracted by dehumanizing them.

The week after it happened, I wrote about Paw West Donezo in a *Jezebel* article about trolling. I wrote sadly, candidly, angrily, with obvious pain.

A few hours after the post went up, I got an email:

*Hey Lindy,*

*I don't know why or even when I started trolling you. It wasn't because of your stance on rape jokes. I don't find them funny either.*

*I think my anger towards you stems from your happiness with your own being. It offended me because it served to highlight my unhappiness with my own self.*

*I have emailed you through 2 other gmail accounts just to send you idiotic insults.*

*I apologize for that.*

*I created the PaulWestDunzo@gmail.com account & Twitter account. (I have deleted both)*

*I can't say sorry enough.*

*It was the lowest thing I had ever done. When you included it in your latest Jezebel article it finally hit me.*

*There is a living, breathing human being who is reading this shit. I am attacking someone who never harmed me in any way. And for no reason whatsoever.*

*I'm done being a troll.*

*Again I apologize.*

*I made a donation in memory to your dad.*

*I wish you the best.*

He attached a receipt for a fifty-dollar donation to Seattle Cancer Care Alliance, designated 'Memorial Paul West' for 'Area of greatest need'.

This email still unhinges my jaw every time I read it. A troll apologizing – this had never happened to me before, it has never happened to me since, I do not know anyone to which it has happened, nor have I heard of such a thing in the wide world of Internet lore. I have read interviews with scholars who study trolling from an academic perspective, specifically stating that the one thing you never get from a troll is public remorse.

I didn't know what to say. I said:

*Is this real? If so, thank you.*

*It was really hurtful, but I'm truly sorry for whatever you've been going through that made you feel compelled to do those things. I wish you the best. And thank you for the donation – it means a lot. I love my dad very much.*

He wrote to me one more time, our final contact:

> *Yes it's true. Thank you for responding with more*
> *kindness than I deserve.*
> *I'm sorry for your loss and any pain I caused you.*
>
> > All the best,
> > [REDACTED] (my real name)

I returned to my regular routine of daily hate mail, scrolling through the same options over and over – Ignore? Block? Report? Engage? – but every time I faced that choice, I thought briefly of my remorseful troll. I wondered if I could learn anything from him, what he'd tell me to do, if he had really changed. And then it struck me – oh my God. I still had his email address. I could just ask him. Even if he turned out to be a jerk, it would make a great story.

I sent the email. After a few months of torturous waiting, he finally wrote back. 'I'd be happy to help you out in any way possible,' he said.

Within a few days, there I was in a recording studio with a phone – and the troll on the other end. We recorded it for *This American Life*, a popular public radio show.

I asked him why he chose me. In his email he wrote that it wasn't because of the rape joke thing, so what exactly did I do?

His voice was soft, tentative. He was clearly as nervous as I was. 'Well,' he said, 'it revolved around one issue that you wrote about a lot which was your being heavy – the struggles that you had regarding being a woman of size, or whatever the term may be.'

I cut in. I hate euphemisms. What the fuck is a 'woman of size', anyway? Who doesn't have a size? 'You can say fat. That's what I say.'

'Fat. Okay, fat.'

He told me that at the time he was about seventy-five pounds heavier than he wanted to be. He hated his body. He was miserable. And reading about fat people, particularly fat women, accepting and loving themselves as they were, infuriated him for reasons he couldn't articulate at the time.

'When you talked about being proud of who you are and where you are and where you're going,' he continued, 'that kind of stoked that anger that I had.'

'Okay,' I said, 'so you found my writing. You found my writing, and you did not like it.'

'Certain aspects of it.'

'Yeah.'

'You used a lot of all caps,' he said. I laughed, and it got him to laugh a little too. 'You're just a very – you almost have no fear when you write. You know, it's like you stand on the desk and you say, "I'm Lindy West, and this is what I believe in. Fuck you if you don't agree with me." And even though you don't say those words exactly, I'm like, who is this bitch who thinks she knows everything?'

I asked him if he felt that way because I'm a woman.

He didn't even hesitate. 'Oh, definitely. Definitely. Women are being more forthright in their writing. There isn't a sense of timidity to when they speak or when they write. They're saying it loud. And I think that – and I think, for me, as well, it's threatening at first.'

'Right.' It was a relief to hear him admit it. So many men cling to the lie that misogyny is a feminist fiction, and rarely do I get such explicit validation that my work is accomplishing exactly what I'm aiming for. 'You must know that I – that's why I do that, because people don't expect to hear from women like that. And I want other women to see me do that and I want women's voices to get louder.'

'I understand,' he said. 'I understand.' I really felt like he did. 'Here's the thing,' he went on. 'I work with women all day, and I don't have an issue with anyone. I could've told you back then if someone had said to me, "Oh, you're a misogynist. You hate women." And I could say, "Nuh-uh, I love my mom. I love my sisters. I've loved my – the girlfriends that I've had in my life." But you can't claim to be okay with women and then go online and insult them – seek them out to harm them emotionally.'

In my experience, if you call a troll a misogynist, he'll almost invariably say, 'Oh, I don't hate women. I just hate what you're saying and what that other woman is saying and that woman and that one for totally unrelated reasons.' So it was satisfying at least to hear him admit that, yeah, he hated women.

We talked for two and a half gruelling hours. They flew by, but every second hurt. He was shockingly self-aware. He said he didn't troll any more, that he'd really changed. He told me that period of time when he was trolling me for being loud and fat was a low point for him. He hated his body. His girlfriend dumped him. He spent every day in front of a computer at an unfulfilling job. A passionless life, he called it. For some reason, he found it 'easy' to take that out on women online.

I asked why. What made women easy targets? In retrospect, I wish I'd been even more plain: Why was it so satisfying to hurt us? Why didn't he automatically see us as human beings? For all his self-reflection, that's the one thing he never managed to articulate – how anger at one woman translated into hatred of women in general. Why, when men hate themselves, it's women who take the beatings.

He did explain how he changed. He started taking care of his health, he found a new girlfriend, and he went back to school to become a teacher. He told me – in all seriousness – that, as a volunteer at a school, *he just gets so many hugs now*. 'Seeing how their feelings get hurt by their peers,' he said, 'on purpose or not, it derails them for the rest of the day. They'll have their head on their desk and refuse to talk. As I'm watching this happen, I can't help but think about the feelings that I hurt.' He was so sorry, he said.

Finally, I brought up my dad.

'How did you even find out that my dad died? How did you –' I trailed off as my voice broke. He saved me the trouble of finishing the question.

'I went to my computer. I Googled you – found out you had a father who had passed. I found out that he had – you had siblings. I forget if it was three total.'

'I have two siblings.'

'So –'

'Did you read his obituary?'

'I believe I did,' he said. 'I knew he was a musician.'

'Yeah, I wrote that.' My voice started to crack; the rapport I'd felt started to harden. 'I wrote his obituary.'

He hesitated at the edge in my voice. 'I created a fake Gmail account using your father's name, created a fake Twitter account using his name. The biography was something to the effect of, my name is – I'm sorry, I forget the name – the first name.'

'His name was Paul West.'

'I wrote, "My name is Paul West. I've got three kids. Two of them are great, and one of them is –"' He hesitated again. ' "An idiot." '

'Yeah, you said "embarrassed father of an idiot." '

'Okay.'

' "Other two kids are fine, though." '

He exhaled. 'Ohhh, that's much more worse.'

'And you got a picture of him,' I said.

'I did get a picture of him.'

'Do you remember anything about him?' I was crying

at this point. 'Did you get a sense of him as a human being?'

'I read the obit. And I knew he was a dad that loved his kids.'

'How did that make you feel?' I wasn't going to be cruel, but I wasn't going to let him off easy either.

'Not good,' he said. 'I mean, I felt horrible almost immediately afterwards. You tweeted something along the lines of, "Good job today, society," or something along those lines. It just wouldn't – for the first time, it wouldn't leave my mind. Usually, I would put out all of this Internet hate, and oftentimes I would just forget about it. This one would not leave me. It would not leave me. I started thinking about you because I know you had read it. And I'm thinking how would she feel. And the next day I wrote you.'

'Yeah,' I whispered, 'I mean, have you lost anyone? Can you imagine? *Can you imagine?*'

'I can. I can. I don't know what else to say except that I'm sorry.'

He sounded defeated. I believed him. I didn't mean to forgive him, but I did.

'Well, you know,' I said, 'I get abuse all day every day. It's part of my job. And this was the meanest thing anyone's ever done to me. I mean, it was really fresh. He had just died. But you're also the only troll who's ever apologized. Not just to me, I've never heard of this happening before. I mean, I don't know anyone who's ever gotten an apology. And I just – I mean, thank you.'

'I'm glad that you have some solace.' He seemed surprised, and relieved, that I hadn't been more cruel. But I was just tired. I didn't have much anger left. We exchanged a few pleasantries, I thanked him, he thanked me, and we hung up.

It felt really easy, comfortable even, to talk to my troll. I liked him, and I didn't know what to do with that.

It's frightening to discover that he's so normal. He has female coworkers who enjoy his company. He has a real, human girlfriend who loves him. They have no idea that he used to go online and traumatize women for fun. How can both of those people share the same brain?

Trolls live among us. I've had anonymous comments from people saying they met me at a movie theatre and I was a bitch. Or they served me at a restaurant and my boobs aren't as big as they look in pictures. Or they sat next to me at a bar five years ago and here is a list of every single bite of food I consumed. People say it doesn't matter what happens on the Internet, that it's not real life. But thanks to Internet trolls, I'm perpetually reminded that the boundary between the civilized world and our worst selves is just an illusion.

Trolls still waste my time and tax my mental health on a daily basis, but honestly, I don't wish them any pain. Their pain is what got us here in the first place.

If what he said is true, that he just needed to find some meaning in his life, then what a heartbreaking diagnosis for all of the people who are still at it. I can't give purpose and fulfilment to millions of anonymous strangers, but I can remember not to lose sight of their humanity the way that they lost sight of mine.

Humans can be reached. I have proof.

This story isn't prescriptive. It doesn't mean that anyone is obliged to forgive people who abuse them, or even that I plan on being cordial and compassionate to every teenage boy who pipes up to call me a blue whale.* But, for me, it's changed the timbre of my online interactions – with, for instance, the guy who responded to my radio story by calling my dad a 'faggot'. That guy does not have a good life. Since this conversation with my troll aired on *This American Life*, I've had to report six more Twitter accounts using my father's name and face, one that scolded me for writing about my abortion. 'Why did you kill my grandchild?' it asked. It got easier every time.

It's hard to feel hurt or frightened when you're flooded with pity. It's hard to be cold or cruel when you remember it's hard to be a person.

---

* 'Whale' is the weakest insult ever, by the way. Oh, I have a giant brain and rule the sea with my majesty? What have you accomplished lately, Steve?

# Abortion Is Normal, It's Okay to Be Fat, and Women Don't Have to Be Nice to You

Just two weeks after my *This American Life* segment aired, copies of a leaked memo by Twitter's then-CEO Dick Costolo began flooding into my inbox from breathless friends. An employee had posted my piece on an internal forum, where it got the attention of Twitter higher-ups, Costolo himself ultimately responding with this blistering communiqué: 'I'm frankly ashamed of how poorly we've dealt with this issue during my tenure as CEO,' he wrote. 'It's absurd. There's no excuse for it. I take full responsibility for not being more aggressive on this front.'

Then: 'We're going to start kicking these people off right and left and making sure that when they issue their ridiculous attacks, nobody hears them. Everybody on the leadership team knows this is vital.'

'We've sucked at it for years,' Costolo went on. 'We're going to fix it.'

I was floored. Like, literally on the floor, rolling around. Bloggers, activists, and academics had been throwing ourselves against Twitter's opaque interface for years – begging for help, compiling sheaves of data on online abuse, writing heartfelt personal essays and dry clinical analyses – and suddenly, in one stroke, we had their ear. There was a human being behind the bird, and he actually gave a shit.

The jury's still out on the long-term efficacy of Twitter's 'fixes'. It's notoriously difficult, if not impossible, to retroactively change a community once bad behaviour has taken root – once users know how to exploit a system, it's hard to evict them without rebuilding the system itself from scratch. Still, to know that Twitter is aware and they're trying – to have the CEO publicly throw his hat in with the feminazis rather than the trolls – is a victory, and a sign that our culture is slowly heaving its bulk in the right direction.

Decisive victories are rare in the culture wars, and the fact that I can count three in my relatively short career – three tangible cultural shifts to which I was lucky enough to contribute – is what keeps me in this job. There's Costolo and the trolls, of course. Then, rape jokes. Comedians are more cautious now, whether they like it or not, while only the most credulous fool or contrarian liar would argue that comedy has no misogyny problem. 'Hello, I

Am Fat' chipped away at the notion that you can 'help' fat people by mocking and shaming us. We talk about fatness differently now than we did five years ago – fat people are no longer safe targets – and I hope I did my part.

All of those changes are small, but they tell us something big: Our world isn't fixed, the way those currently in charge would have you believe. It's malleable.

When I was a little girl, I was obsessed with a video-game developer named Roberta Williams. She made point-and-click adventure games – King's Quest, Space Quest, Quest for Glory – a largely extinct genre in which exploration, curiosity, and problem solving took precedence over combat and reflexes. As a corny king or a dopey spaceman, you wandered through brilliant, interactive landscapes, picking up random shit in the hope that it might help you rescue a pissed-off gnome from a swarm of bees, or break a talking collie out of dog prison so he'll reward you with the magic kerchief you need to blindfold the King of the Dead.

I wanted to be Roberta Williams; I wanted to build worlds.

In ninth grade, I enrolled in a beginners' programming class at a community college near my house. I was the youngest one there, the only girl, and the only one with no previous knowledge of coding (which wasn't a prerequisite); the teacher ignored me and chattered away with the boys in jargon I couldn't follow. I sat through two classes in a humiliated, frustrated fog and never went back. I drifted away from video games; they didn't want me. I forgot about Roberta and grew up.

I think the most important thing I do in my professional life today is delivering public, impermeable 'no's and sticking to them. I say no to people who prioritize being cool over being good. I say no to misogynists who want to weaponize my body against me. I say no to men who feel entitled to my attention and reverence, who treat everything the light touches as a resource for them to burn. I say no to religious zealots who insist that I am less important than an embryo. I say no to my own instinct to stay quiet.

Nah, no thanks, I'm good, bye. Ew, don't talk to me. Fuck off.

It's a way of kicking down the boundaries that society has set for women – be compliant, be a caregiver, be quiet – and erecting my own. I will do this; I will not do that. You believe in my subjugation; I don't have to be nice to you. I am busy; my time is not a public commodity. You are boring; go away.

That is world-building.

My little victories – trolls, rape jokes, fat people's humanity – are world-building. Fighting for diverse voices is world-building. Proclaiming the inherent value of fat people is world-building. Believing rape victims is world-building. Refusing to cave to abortion stigma is world-building. Voting is world-building. So is kindness, compassion, listening, making space, saying yes, saying no.

We're all building our world, right now, in real time. Let's build it better.

# Acknowledgements

First, to the Wests and the Oluos. I am so lucky.

To my mom, Ingrid, for teaching me that there's a right way and a wrong way, for taking care of me, and for always following through. To my dad, Paul, for modelling kindness and ebullience, blazing creativity and unconditional love. I miss you. I wish you could have read my book.

To my agent and friend, Gary Morris, who is just the best, for being so patient and encouraging while I figured out WTF a book is. To the whole team at Hachette, especially Mauro DiPreta. It is so fucking cool that you hitched your wagon to this fat feminist abortion manifesto – your confidence in me means everything – and I'm sorry I said 'fart' so many times even after you asked me to pump the brakes on that.

To Paul Constant, Rafil Kroll-Zaidi, Guy Branum, Corianton Hale and Amelia Bonow for the guidance and reassurance. To every member of the Secret Book Writing

Accountability and Crying Group – you are my medicine. To Charlotte and John MacVane for the solitude and whoopie pies. To Hedgebrook for reaching out to me with such supernaturally perfect timing that I almost believe in God now (and/or wiretapping?). To Meagan Hatcher-Mays for being a better version of me. You ate the thirteenth biscuit. To Annie Wagner and Jessica Coen for my big breaks. To Ira Glass and Chana Joffe-Walt. To every fat person who's ever sent me an email. To my *Stranger* family, my GHS family, and my Oxy family. To Tamora Pierce audiobooks and every flavour of Runts except banana.

Thank you.

And to my husband, Ahamefule J. Oluo: You are the best thinker and funniest joke writer and most brilliant artist in the whole world, but you're an even better partner. I love you, I love you, I love you.